I Want to Sing Your Song

40 Day Daily Devotional (Verse and Song)

Written & Compiled by

Alitta P.S Cadmus & Melissea M Walters

I Want to Sing Your Song
Copyright © 2020 by Alitta P.S Cadmus & Melissea M Walters

Tellwell Talent
www.tellwell.ca

ISBN
978-0-2288-4079-4 (Hardcover)
978-0-2288-4078-7 (Paperback)

Acknowledgement

Writing this acknowledgement would take an entire chapter, but to give it justice, we would like to take this time to acknowledge everyone who has played a role to support, pray and push for this book to be completed. We do not know where to even begin. Saying thank you is hardly sufficient; nevertheless, this book would never have been possible if it weren't for the words of encouragement given by the people who have supported and lifted us up. To our family, church family and friends, we appreciate you for your prayers and support.

We especially want to thank the following individuals who contributed to this book finally coming to fruition

First and foremost, *all* the praise and glory belong to our Lord and saviour, Jesus Christ, the anchor of our soul. If it wasn't for Him, we do not know where we would be. He has always been that light shining at the end, beckoning us to come forward. He has kept us from giving up and throwing in the towel, especially when the temptation presented itself to do so. For the good and bad times, You are ever faithful and always there.

To our parents, as the good book says, we honour you for the Christian values that you have instilled in us. To our mother, Marie R, Vaughan Cadmus; thank you for all the sacrifices you have made to raise and train us into the way, we ought to go. You have always been that voice of strength. Telling us we can do anything we put our minds to. If it wasn't for you reminding us that we are good enough, we do not know if we would have the confidence to finish this book. To Sunday O. Cadmus, (Baba!), thank you for teaching us how to harness and use what God has given us. We would not be who we are today if it were not for you. Thank you for your love and support. And of course - your intelligence has taken root. Love you, Baba!

We specifically want to thank our dear brother John O. Cadmus aka Man of God. The Holy Spirit used you to direct us on this path. Your words of wisdom sparked a light that caught fire, and now the book is finally here. We appreciate you in more ways than one. To our dear brother Michael W. Cadmus: you have inspired us to not settle for less, or ever give up. Thank you for always being there.

To Shola# 1 (Debbie Cadmus). You knew what we needed to get the job done, and you gave it to us no questions asked, and for that, we will forever be grateful.

To Talks with Sosa, thank you for opening the door for us to step through.

To the founding members and the entire organization of the CBLR, we forever grateful to you. You have reignited the light, stirring the fire under our tails, Showing us that Christian authors do matter and most important that we do have a story to tell.

To Natalie Cousins, where do we even begin? You saw the vision and understood it. Even at times when it made no sense, you knew at some point it would have to happen. And you kept calling to make sure we were making the right steps toward success.

To the Faculty of arts at KPU for giving us the tools to learn and harness our craft.

To Bonito Grange, who mentored and encouraged to envision the book being completed and sold.

To Nadia Woollery, who said, "Get it done!"

To everyone who helped and supported this vision, we thank you.

Once again

All praise belongs to God. He is our number ONE supporter through it all. To Him be the glory and praise.

Dedication

In memory of
Peter Grange
Emogene Milton
Winston O'Neil Fisher

In Honor of
Johanna Rosalina Gill Walters
The angel who passed through.

Introduction: What it All Means

The Verse
A line of poetry; a stanza of a poem; a short
section of a chapter in the Bible [1]

The Song
Responds to the poem (the verse) with a melody

How it Came Together?
Over the ages, God has blessed mankind with the ability and the
lyrical gift to sing praises unto Him. From the book of Psalms, David
emphasizes "*O sing unto the Lord a new song: sing unto the Lord, all the
earth. Sing unto the Lord, bless his name; shew forth his salvation from day
to day*" (Psalms 96:1).

Music, in its totality, is embedded in the fabric of most cultures across
the social spectrum. It is how we harness the ingenuity to tell the stories
that matter, and add value to who we are. It is how we are able to harness
and maintain the history of where we come from, and what we all strive
to be. t is about telling a message, and generating a joy that runs deep to
the soles of dancing feet.

For "I Want to Sing Your Song" it has been a long time coming. How
it came to be, could be a long story, but we will give you the short version.
Both of us grew up in the church, surrounded by the culture of spiritual
hymns and songs. We started to write songs to express what we understood
about God and our Christian walk. Inspired by gospel music in all its
forms, we penned songs, not fully understanding what we created. After
developing, and cultivating a passion to sing for God, it was confirmed
that this gift of ministry was commission and given by God. Coming from
different creative abilities, we came together to join our gifts of poetry

(verse) and song into a devotional of edification and enlightenment. The concept was originally birthed from a song. It was an expression of our heart that we wanted to sing songs that pleased the Lord, but equally ministered to the soul. Of his unique nature and sovereignty, God has a way of communicating with his children. For the situations we have faced before and after writing this book, the Lord has ministered to our hearts with hymns and songs. Today we present this symbol of our praise to Him as well as you our fellow members in Christ.

Each topic has been carefully selected, addressing the various areas of our daily living. A demonstration of our faith in Christ, the songs and poems express our need to walk with Jesus Christ, our Lord. There is a song that God has placed on the hearts of his people, and it is our liberty to sing them.

There are *40 days* in total and the structure follows:

- A Biblical verse
- A *responding (poem) verse, and song.*
- A Reflection that provides scriptural insight
- Your Own *Reflection* (Note Taking)

You can read the days in order, or however, the Holy Spirit will lead you.

**Today you can sing the Lord's Song, the one He wants to hear.
When you get to the end of all days, may
you <u>Cross Over</u> into the New Life.**

Table of Contents

The Intimacy of My Praise, My Worship

I will bless the Lord at all times: his praise shall continually be in my mouth ♦ **Psalms 34:1**

We will go into his tabernacles: we will worship at his footstool ♦ **Psalms 132:7**

God is a spirit, and they that worship him, must worship him in spirit and truth ♦ **John 4:24**

THE VERSE

Subtle, delicate, strong,
a sound ushers past the gates of my soul.
It is a wave with a wind behind the storm.
Pushing into the heart the arms expand upward,
whilst the Heavens roll the clouds away.

In this realm *Your* unequivocal power unveils the difference between us.
Commanding silence shuts out *what is and should be.*

As you flow through the wave of an endogenous narration,
You flow through the wave of natural expression and ovations.

The *Might* of Your footsteps sound your approach.

What more should I do,
but allow the essence of my spirit
to drum to the rhythm of grace and truth?

An intertwined harmony,
for which fear would want me to fight,
I resolve everything that I am to be still.
On the journey to the secret place, nothing else matters.

Our hands held together, your eyes blend with mine.
In the moment, words no longer carry the burden of expression.
In my speech I align the phrase.
I align the alliteration.
I align the verbs and adjectives.

Together a blended lyric, I sing, I sing praises.
Forever let it be poured out from my bowed heart.
Granting me *this* liberation,
Your song converts my strength.
Upon an exhale, it converts my worship,

Expanding the ribcage, it pushes against the cares of pain.
It pushes against self-fish reasons to resist.

Igniting the dark places, the love molds my praise into what You want.

Churning across the expanse of the tunnel,
it erases suppression and oppression.
Surrounded by Your glory,
may my flesh sit in the palm of humility.

On the altar of sacrifice,
let my body become the symbol of prostrate, an all faded canvas.

In the space where we marry,
there is Your call of Hallelujahs.
As a wife to her husband,
and a husband to his wife, for Your love,
for Your mercy, I lift Your name.

Now Oh Lord.
Now Oh Lord, I confess.
There is nothing more.
There is nothing more, I rather do than to worship You.
There is nothing more that I rather do than to give You Praise.

This is my worship
The language of love.

YOUR SONG

There's nothing more that I rather do than to worship you
There's nothing more that I rather do than to praise you

Oh, Oh, For Your love
And for Your mercy
And for Your grace

I lift up Your name
I lift up Your name
I lift up Your name

There's nothing more that I rather do than to worship You

Reflection

I WILL SING YOUR PRAISE...YOUR WORSHIP
For your love, for your mercy, I lift Your name

A wife looks at her husband. Her vulnerable and unguarded gaze pierces his dark coals while he stares back at her. In this moment of exposed vulnerability, every fiber of her being is to love, nourish, and appreciate the one who has been and is her rock and friend. She cannot deny that the intimacy between them is divine, and she knows deep in her soul, she would not trade him for anything in the world. If she could articulate what she truly feels, it would not be far from an intimate praise and worship. Despite the hard times that have hit them thus far, and while she is uncertain of what the future may hold, she vows within herself not to rob him of the gift to be his wife, nor will she cheat their marriage by giving intimacy to another. As she stands there looking at him, she acknowledges that their love is a ministry - a symbol of glory and praise to their God, who had brought them together.

Just imagine how you would feel when someone you love, focuses their attention solely on you, and speaks with sincerity from their heart? They take the time to acknowledge who you are, and they don't merely say "I love you" but they show and mean it?

Between Jesus, and the church, there is a bond that is similar to the bond shared between a husband and a wife.

Metaphorically described as the bride, the church, has been given this divine access and liberation to worship and praise God. From your heartfelt reverence, it extends from a place of understanding and respect. Esteeming Him above yourself, it is gradually cultivated when you come face to face with the character and qualities of God.

The relationship, between Jesus and the Church (the bride of Christ), involves and is dependent, on how much you know and adore Him. As you would expect sincere appreciation from the people you know and love, Jesus *who you would consider to love*, expects no less.

Of His interaction with the woman of Samaria, Jesus foretold that the method of worship would change; including how it was to be done.

"…But the hour is coming, and now is, when the true worshipers will worship the Father in spirit and truth; for the Father is seeking such to worship Him. God is Spirit, and those who worship Him must worship in spirit and truth" (John 4:21-24b[NKJV]).

True worship, as Jesus explained, extends from the root of a relationship. Hence, if you are to sing God's songs of praise and worship, it means your expression of homage will come from truth. You are honest inwardly, and outwardly. It is a willingness of your heart to be open to the believe of who Jesus is to you.

Just like a wife and husband, when they acknowledge each other with articulated admiration, it has more impact and value when it is true. The husband feels appreciated and valuable, which compels him to do more for his wife than she usually asks of him. The wife feels special and worthy, which compels her to do more for her husband than he asks of her. The magnitude of their love and commitment opens the door of their heart and spirit to transparency, and obeisance. Unlike rendered flattery, genuine praise and authentic worship compels God to respond in kind. He will bless you with a word of strength. He will shower you with his love of blessings: both physical and spiritual.

For your praise, and for your worship, you can lift His name [Jehovah] knowing who He is, and He knows [you]".

TODAY YOU CAN SING THE LORD'S SONG "I LIFT UP YOUR NAME"

Scripture Reference
**Psalms 34:1 ♦ Psalm 150 John 4:21-24 ♦
Psalms 101:1 ♦ Psalms 132:7**

I Want to Sing Your Song

Your Day's Reflection

_____

_____

_____

_____

_____

_____

_____

_____

You Give Me Joy

Thou wilt shew me the path of life: in thy presence is fullness of joy; at thy right hand there are pleasures for evermore. ◆ **Psalm 16:11**

But the fruit of the Spirit is love, joy, peace, long suffering, gentleness, goodness, faith
◆ **Galatians 5:22**

These things have I spoken unto you, that my joy might remain in you, and that your joy might be full. ◆ **John 15:11**

THE VERSE

You give me joy in the morning
to face the dawn of a new breath.
It is never earned,
but the beauty and the tenderness of your compassion, brushes the soul.
I am awake; I am whole.

In Your presence,
I am surrounded by the fullness of contentment.
And I 'am enfolded in the peace to know You are there.

I can rejoice, rejoice Oh, my soul
for at Your right hand, there are pleasures for evermore.

The secret of the spirit is to dance in the mist.
It is to look up and envision
the invisible traces of great triumph.

Manifested in praises,
carried on a song,
the aroma fills the atmosphere.

The cares of life discourse
do allude to the possibility of a dreadful loneliness.
As such, the hands labor in water, fire, and storm.
The race to the finish drums the heart.

Nevertheless.

A lesson learned in fellowship;
in gatherings of souls, I can rejoice.
Because the call of all and one,
generates a celebration
to magnify the blessing of living for today.

Placed at my lips, Oh Lord is Your fruit.
I will consume it while I dine at the table of men and women laughing.

The seasons will converge days upon days.
The times will leave no mercy.
The windows of many mornings will collect dust.

While my voice shouts with great adulations,
it is the resting of the thought and believing: *"this too shall pass."*
It is the soles of the feet
persevering in the rain,
as the head is crowned with glory.

When the thorns of the rose inflict the flesh[1],
and the trials of life storm in,

my hope rests on the joy that awaits me in tomorrows.

Rejoice, rejoice Oh my soul.
For every season.
For every morning.
For every moonlight.
This joy contained in the core,
is You Oh Lord, living inside my soul.

YOUR SONG

You give me joy
Joy in the morning
(Joy) in the evening
(Joy) every season
Summer, Winter, Spring, or Fall
(repeat)

Cause without Your love there's no point living
Just to have You in my life is all that matters
And just to hear Your name the atmosphere has changed
Cause when I think of all Your goodness You give me…joy

You give me joy
Joy in the morning
(Joy) in the evening
(Joy) every season
Summer, Winter, Spring, or Fall

Reflection

*Like praise and worship, joy, when you come to grips of
what it is, and the value it adds to life, many would say
it is not something they ever want to live without.*

Naturally, when you feel an abundance of happiness, it is virtually attributed to feelings of immense delight for what is happening and will happen. It is without question most people want to experience and feel happy all the time. For no one wakes up in the morning hoping for something bad to happen. Or desiring to feel misery. Through small, and even great series of events, you will yearn to live in the moments of great bliss. This is lent to the fact that internally, you feel a gladness that ignites you to feel good about life, and all it has to offer. And when it does not last long, your moments of jubilee are not far from being a gift; a precious moment in time cherished for when *you will not feel so happy.*

**For the seasons you go through, joy can
come just by being in the presence
of those who can arouse you to laugh, dance clap and sing.**

David, a man after God's own heart - historically, a great poet and psalmist - went through a lot for which he was inspired to write majority of the psalms out of the 150 in the Bible. The timeline of his life reveal how he came to pen: *"Thou wilt shew me the path of life: in thy presence is fulness of joy; at thy right hand there are pleasures for evermore"* (Psalm 16:11).

Before he became a King of prominence, he was a lowly shepherd tending to His father's sheep. Some would say he lived an okay life without the worries that came after he was anointed by Samuel. He encountered a giant, faced jealousy, death, and experienced a great loss. From his own mistakes, he had to deal with the devastation of judgement in his home. Yet, through it all, he discovered an unspeakable joy in the presence of God.

**Has there been a time in your life that despite everything,
you still felt the joy of the Lord flood your heart?**

Completely opposite of joy, there are moments when everything that is happening around and in you does not feel right. You are faced with gigantic goliaths that threaten your livelihood. At home things seem to be going far left than right. Temptations of all kinds test your dignity and integrity. It is only a matter of time before you lose it. The devastation of your mistakes on top of everything else invites depression, and suppression to overshadow. You do try to muster some courage but each step forward, only seems like ten steps backward.

Jesus who truly understands what it is to feel heartache and grief, encourages believers saying,

"These things have I spoken unto you, that my joy might remain in you, and that your joy might be full" (John 15:11).

In line with the context of abiding in Him, Jesus identifies himself as the True Vine, and he reassures that " … *He that abideth in me, and I in him, the same bringeth forth much fruit: for without me ye can do nothing"* (John 15:5).

The joy, for which *Jesus* speaks of comes from the Heavenly Father (God). It is found in His presence, and with the companionship of His word. As situations around you will seem impossible, and it makes sense to give up there is a joy which lingers beneath the veneer of pain and sorrow. A joy for which no man can give, and no man can take away.

*From the seasons of life, you can look to … "the horizon and know
this joy contained in the core," is the Yahweh "living inside [your] soul."*

TODAY YOU CAN SING THE LORD'S SONG "YOU GIVE ME
JOY: SUMMER WINTER, SPRING OR FALL"

Scripture Reference
**John 15:11 ♦ Psalm 16:11 ♦ Romans 15:13
♦ Psalms 16:11 ♦ Psalms 30:5**

I Want to Sing Your Song

Your Day's Reflection

_____

_____

_____

_____

_____

_____

_____

_____

_____

The Quiet Place

A time to rend, and a time to sew; a time to keep silence,
and a time to speak ♦ **Ecclesiastes 3:7**

And in the morning, rising up a great while before day, he went out,
and departed into a solitary place, and there prayed. ♦ **Mark 1:16**

And on the seventh day God ended his work which he
had made; and he rested on the seventh day from all
his work which he had made. ♦ **Genesis 2:2**

THE VERSE

It is not wrong, for this is right.
Cease from the noise which spreads abroad
and crosses back again.

Rest awhile.
Be still.
Settle here.

When I settle here,
the silence is the altogether grace,
upon which the head is cocooned.
It is framed between the moment of
here and now.

The constant pulling is at ease,
and the abundance of reflection,
mirrors the wounds of which the eyes cannot see.

When the time has come,
this is the chance to convene
with the Holy Spirit.

I can bow at Jehovah Shalom's [1] feet.
I can wear my garment, worn and torn.
In the solitude, it is appreciated for its tatters.

That which I've held unto for so long,
I can brace the handles of strength to let them be and to let them go.

The noise of horns, abounding from many, one
and all, will always want attention.
The ears will itch for the noise of the city.
It combines with the pouring out; it is the truth of labor.

The mouth will always labour for what it will eat.
The eyes will seek to cry for visions of hope.
The feet will always attempt the line of giving,
till the soles know the ground to the dirt.

From all, I've seen.
All I know.
I still need to withdraw into the silence
where the quiet becomes the opportunity to
see what the ears cannot hear.

It is the hum of the ballad which tells the story
of God's love and compelling salvation.

It is such a burden of the racing blood which toils for the exhale.

In my voice, the cries wild for the night.

Lord, Oh Lord, take me to the Shaqat.[2]
Let me be the Shalem.[3]

It is not wrong, for this is right.
I cease from the noise, which spreads abroad and crosses back again.

I Enter the quiet place.
Resting awhile.
Being still.
Settling here.

YOUR SONG

No Distractions
All other voices be still
Mind, body, spirit
All must be centered on You
Lord Let me hear You
So I can walk the way of truth
And my mind be renewed

In that quiet place is where I need to be
In your presence,
Jesus just You and me
In Your Presence is where I love to be
In that quiet
In that quiet place.

Reflection

I WILL SING FOR THE SHAQAT...FOR NUWACH
In that quiet place is where I need to be

When was the last time you had a moment to yourself, and you could actually hear yourself think? When was the last time you stood before a sunset, and you could listen to the lull of nothing? When you woke up this morning, after a long or short night of sleeping, what was the first thing on your mind? Did you open your eyes and embrace the day with a quiet calm? Or did your thoughts carry you on a marathon of chores and things that need your immediate attention? Whatever the case might be, the thing that is of utmost importance, is your acknowledgment of what you might've denied yourself: *a moment of silence and a place of quiet.*

There is so much in this world that vie for your attention. There is a labour that demands for more than it gives. While these varying aspects are important in their own value, weight, and time, it is essential to understand when it is time to stop, pause and have a moment to think. For it is in the quiet moments when you can gather your thoughts, and gain clarity about the situations you have to deal with from day to day.

There is time for everything. A time to do,
a time to see and a time to act
(Ecclesiastes 3:7).

When Jesus walked this earth, He was committed to the ministry of redemption. He spent a significant amount of time amongst his disciples, teaching and preparing them for things to come. Throngs and masses of people followed Him. He healed the sick, raised the dead, fed the poor and, most importantly, preached the message of salvation. Powerful, dedicated, and focused as Jesus was, there did come a moment when He needed to be alone. He needed a time of silence, meditation, and rejuvenation.

Coming up to the time when He would be crucified, scripture tells us that "... *before daylight, He went out and departed to a solitary place; and there He prayed*" (Mark 1:35b).

In the beginning of creation, after God took His time to create everything, He rested on *"the seventh day"*. He then *"blessed"* and *"sanctified it"* (Genesis 2:1-3).

Ordinarily, it is natural to become exhausted and nothing is wrong when you feel tired. But, when it is time to rest, it is important to recognize the signs when you need to get away.

As you transcend from the realms of slumber, your mind will begin to calculate the variety of things you have to do. It will process, the situations to address, the deadlines and goals you want (and or need) to meet. While these priorities and activities are significant to living, it is essential to take into consideration, how such incidences can sometimes cause you to lose sight of what is important. Your voice can get lost in the shuffle, and you could be doing and saying a lot. The lingering question then becomes: *"Can I hear my own voice. Can I hear myself think? Can I hear God's Voice?"*

If the answer is not clear, it possibly means that it is time to pause. It is time to get away.

There is nothing wrong in taking the time to escape into a solitary place to pray. There is nothing wrong in taking the time to soothe your weary mind and body.

...for this is right.
Cease from the noise which spreads abroad and crosses back again.

Rest awhile.
Be still.
Settle here.

Today you can sing the Lord's song "In that quiet place is where I need to be"

Scripture Reference
Ecclesiastes 3:7 ♦ Mark 1:36 ♦ Genesis 2:2

Your Day's Reflection

_____

_____

_____

_____

_____

_____

_____

_____

_____

Holy Spirit Rain Down on Me

Now the Lord is that Spirit: and where the
Spirit of the Lord is, there is liberty.
♦ **1 Corinthians 3:17**

But the Comforter, which is the Holy Ghost, whom the Father
will send in my name, he shall teach you all things, and bring all
things to your remembrance, whatsoever I have said unto you.
♦ **John 14:26**

For as many as are led by the Spirit of God, they are the sons of God...
♦ **Romans 8:14-16.**

THE VERSE

Holy Spirit, and Comforter
your morning rains are the new mercies
which allow for new growth and new life.
Under the firmament of the heavens,
Your essence is glorified in us.

Before you, I stand open and free.
"Holy Spirit, let Your love rain down on me."

Rain down on me, Your truth.
Rain down on me, Your song.

I Want to Sing Your Song

Rest Your substance upon my entire being.
Let the emblems of fire embed in my flesh.

From the cries of my spirit, I shout out the deliverance.
Holy Spirit, Holy Spirit flood me so

Unto holiness, You Call.
Unto righteousness, You lead.
In the consciousness of such power,
the brotherly love is exalted.

In the spirit, I can see the path expanded for my feet to stay in the way.
With jewels, of love, forgiveness, and mercy,
the soul is adorned with the power to forsake wrath.

Revealer of truth.
Exposer of deceits.
In Sovereignty, You give.
In Authority, You give grace.

Holy Spirit, Holy Spirit, let Your love rain down on me."
Rain down on me, Your truth.
Rain down on me, Your song.
With my hands stretched forth,
I position the left and right.
Forming them into a palm to receive
and
accept the drink from this well.

With tarried tears, and tarried hands,
My head is lifted, and my faith is awakened.

Voice of creation.
The Maker of unions.
Giver of seeds and seas,
rain down, rain down on me.

Holy Spirit, Holy Spirit, let Your love rain down on me."

Your Song

Holy Spirit let Your love rain down on me
Refill me with Your precious life anew
Gently rest upon me softly as the morning dew
Abundantly restore every substance of peace and truth

Rain on me, Jesus let Your Spirit rain on me
Rain on me, Jesus let Your Spirit rain on me

Let the windows of heaven open up and rain on me today
I feel joy in Your presence
I surrender myself, and I give You my heart today

Rain on me, Jesus let your Spirit rain on me
Rain on me, Jesus let You Spirit rain on me

Reflection

Imagine you are standing under the abundance of a torrential downpour. It is like a curtain, descending all over your body, drenching every part of you. The muted sound drowns out every other clamor. All that is left for you to do is to let go and bask in the exhilarating blessings of nature.

Now imagine, this is the Holy-Spirit raining down His aura, power, liberty, peace, and calm over you. It engulfs the perimeters of where you stand. This unexplainable phenomenon replaces the thoughts racing in your mind. The traffics of life's expectancy fade away into the far distance, and absolutely nothing matters to you than this very moment.

Not your finances or health concerns. Not the questions pounding through your mind. Not the abjection of your mistakes. Not the pain of betrayal or rejection. Absolutely nothing matters for this hour.

God promised to pour out His Spirit on all flesh.

Explaining who and what the Holy Spirit is, Jesus says: *"But the Comforter, which is the Holy Ghost, whom the Father will send in my name, he shall teach you all things, and bring all things to your remembrance..."* (John 14:26-27).

On the Day of Pentecost as promised:

"...they were all with one accord in one place. And suddenly there came a sound from heaven, as of a rushing mighty wind, and it filled the whole house where they were sitting. Then there appeared to them [b]divided tongues, as of fire, and one sat upon each of them. And they were all filled with the Holy Spirit and began to speak with other tongues, as the Spirit gave them utterance" (Acts 2:1-4a).

Like a power source, the purpose of the Holy Spirit is to reconnect you back to God (the Creator) and empower you. With such power, you can live the way God wants you to. You can do the things you would not normally do on your own. As a Spirit is beyond human comprehension, somethings cannot be explained nor understood by human (flesh) intellect. Through Jesus, who is that Holy Spirit living in you, He is that voice you will often hear in your subconscious; revealing truth and that which are lies.

In His word, it is promised, *"In the last days"* He will *"pour out"* of His Spirit on *"all flesh."* You the *"sons and daughters shall prophesy... dream dreams, and... shall see visions"* (Act 2:17a-b).

At the appointed time, when Holy Spirit is upon
you, all that will be left for you to do is:

...Bow before Him.
Be open and free...
let [His] love rain down on you"
Let Him rain down His truth.
Let Him Rain down the song that will flood your soul.

Today you can sing the Lord's song: "Holy
Spirit let Your love rain down on me"

Scripture Reference
Genesis 1:2 ♦ John 16:7-8 ♦ Acts 2:17 ♦ Romans
8:10-11 ♦ 1 Corinthians 3:17 ♦ John 14:16

Your Day's Reflection

Just Be with Me

I am the vine, ye are the branches: He that abideth in me, and I in him,
the same bringeth forth much fruit: for without me ye can do nothing.
♦ ***John 15:5***

He who dwells in the secret place of the Most High
Shall abide under the shadow of the Almighty.
♦ **Psalms 91:1**

Behold, I stand at the door and knock. If anyone hears My
voice and opens the door, I will come into him and dine
with him, and he with Me. ♦ **Revelation 3:20**

THE VERSE

Wake up my child; it is morning.
Can you hear me knocking?
Come open this door;
I want to be with thee.

Do not overthink it.
Open the door, and let me step in.

Let me come and be in your heart.
So, when the course of terror and despair, overwhelm to take you down,
My shield will be your hiding place from the flying sorrows.

Take my hand and try to understand.
You do not have to pull back, nor be afraid.
I will not harm you.
I will not deceive nor put up a front.
My words are sound and true.

Set your sights upon my Face and hear My Voice.
Listen, listen closely.
Understand the quality and be attune to the sincerity.

What I say, what I speak is complete.
It shall accomplish that which it has been set forth to do.

Once it has traversed the earth,
looking for a dwelling place to carry out its mission,
it cannot return to me void.

Forget the sayings of impossibility.
Trust Me when I say, "It is finished."

Come, come, come from out of the past
and Just Be with Me.

I see and hear your constant means.
I want to heal you from your angry deeds.

Willfully, with all my love, I nailed this body to
redemption. A solemn kiss and vow, I planted it on your
pain. It has sealed the fate of my everlasting Grace.

While I pleaded for another way.
I could not renounce.
I could not suspend, for this had to happen in the end.

It had to happen for the valley and the grief.
It happened for your storms and the nation's burdens.

Catapults by stones, I saw it all.
I see YOU.

By your bedside, when all is quiet, and loneliness evades
like a shadow creeping underfoot, I see you.

At your sink-side when the cares,
the issues and leftovers of this life descend and surround
I am there.

Many will betray.
Many will bless.

Many will reject.
Many will despise.

Many will kill.
Lie.
Steal.
Humiliate you.
But I the Lord, I am not like man.
Come … come … come,
just be with me.
And I will always be there.

YOUR SONG

Just be with me
Come, come, let me embrace you in my arms
Just be with me, I will keep you from all harm
Just be with me
No need,
No need to fear
Just be with me, and I'll always be there

(There) I'll always be there
Just be with me, and I'll always be there.

Reflection

I will sing: For I Know You are There
You will embrace me, in your arms

Similar to you taking the time to rest and rejuvenate from the busyness of life, it is equally necessary when you can take the time and spend it with the people you know and love. Defined as "quality time," it can be quite beneficial for strengthening the bonds within your relationships. The benefits include the elements needed to maintain, the love, joy, and peace that you share amongst yourself. With relatability, you get to learn new things about each other. During such times, there is a commendable satisfaction, that soothes your being, when you are in the presence of those you care about. There are no conditions or limitations. Regardless of the times and/issues, their presence can lift your spirit and make you feel safe. This type of company can predominantly be with either a close friend or a beloved family member. The occasion could also be for a formal and or casual setting. Within yourself, you will appreciate the joy and laughter, ignited by jovial conversations. From hugs and kisses, you will feel much better knowing, this time spent together was worth it. There will be the days when they will call you and say

"*Let us just have this day together, no noise, no formalities, let's just be in each other's company, and enjoy the day.*" And, for every day missed, you will look forward to the time when you can meet again.

While you will be absorbed into the discourse and noise of this life, the Holy Spirit will still beckon to you to come and be with Him.

At the beginning of time, during the cool of the day, the Spirit of the Lord's voice could be heard walking in the garden. The presence of his voice signified how He was taking the time to dwell amongst His creation. Despite Adam & Eve's disobedience of eating the forbidden fruit, God still covered them, which demonstrated how much he loved and cared for them. After the act of redemption, through Jesus, God reestablished the connection.

Within your circle of friends, there will be times when your fellowship gets disrupted. Something minor or major happens, and you isolate yourself from one another. For Adam and Eve, this was their situation because God had to now put them out of his physical presence. While His grace was clearly with them, the fellowship they once had was different. Their *"quality time"* was different.

Jesus chastens after those He loves.

For the church in Laodicea, their quality time with Jesus was almost nonexistent, and He was not pleased with how they were neither here nor there. (Not hot or cold). However, through His mercy and love, in the latter part of His message He said,

"As many as I love, I rebuke and chasten! Therefore, be zealous and repent. Behold, I stand at the door and knock. If anyone hears My voice and opens the door, I will come into him and dine with him, and he with Me" (Revelation 3:19-20).

For most relationships, like the one between you and Jesus, quality time serves as that anchor to remind you of what that person means to you. Because when intrusion comes to cause division, those precious moments you would have spent together, would serve as a reminder. It would be like a string to pull you back to what is important. You gain strength to know, the problems and strive are not worth it. When you spend "quality time", and abide in the presence of the Lord, you receive joy and "pleasures forever more" (Psalm 16:11b). You receive hope, healing, and strength to carry on. You gain access to God's throne for sweet communion. *"...in the secret place of the Most High,* [you] *shall abide under the shadow of the Almighty.* [you] *will say of the Lord, 'He is my refuge and my fortress; My God, in Him I will trust.'"* (Psalm 91: 1-2).

> *"Come open this door; I want to be with thee.*
> *Do not overthink it.*
> *Open the door, and let me step in."*

TODAY YOU CAN SING THE LORD'S SONG "JUST BE
WITH ME, AND I'LL ALWAYS BE THERE"

Scripture Reference
John 15:5 ♦ Genesis 3:8 ♦ Exodus 33:14

Your Day's Reflection

_____

_____

_____

_____

_____

_____

_____

_____

_____

Where Can I Find You

Seek ye the Lord while he may be found, call ye upon him while he is near
♦ Isaiah 55:6

I love them that love me; and those that seek me early shall find me
♦ Proverbs 8:17

Then shall ye call upon me, and ye shall go and pray
unto me, and I will hearken unto you.
And ye shall seek me, and find me, when ye shall
search for me with all your heart.
♦ Jeremiah 29:12-13

THE VERSE

Seek ye the Lord.
Call ye upon Him.
Near, near He is and this
I must achieve.

I close my eyes away,
from the attraction of this world.
While the rain falls like tiny droplets
flooding streams and creeks,
I walk through the sea of people
who carry burdens to lay at Your feet.

I wonder and wonder to myself,
Where, oh where Lord will I find Thee?

Singing Your name while beating my chest,
I stand at junctures pulling in every direction.
There are choices on every hand.
Yet, as I glean on principles of contextually
I am not sure of the greatest outcome.

I am not sure of what I believe.
I am not sure of what is seen,
heard, or spoken of.

Placed on the scale,
the soul weighs in the balance
I consider,
I pray,
I seek.
Where, oh where Lord do I find Thee?

In my heart, soul, spirit and entire being,
pray, pray, I do.
My spirit lifts to hearken unto You.
No matter what I do, wherever I go,
I know I must find You.

Tug and pull.
I am drafted by the flesh, for it has its conquest
I feel the pull to lay and wait.

In the abundance of salt and sea, my feet tickle for peace.

I was a captive in a closed-off realm,
surrounded by hums of temporal cares.
The voice became absorbed by the jingling of the ruthless.

It rested against the vision that somehow, someday it is found.

Deep, deep, down,
a cry still bellows across the halls of the soul.
It appeals from hollowness.

This is the love I need,
This is the love I want.

As I seek for Thee,
I sing for You and write the songs of Yahweh.
Where, oh, where do I find thee?

Lord if You hear my cry,
and while I do have time,
let me find Thee.

YOUR SONG

Where Can I find You?
How will I know that it's You?
Holding my hand
Where will I go?
How will
I survive without You?
I'm lost without You
I can't go on without You

Lord, if You hear my cry and while I do have
the time let me find You (x3)
Let me find You
Let me find You
Let me, let me
Let me find You

Reflection

Have you ever lost a connection with someone you loved, and no matter how much you thought it would get better, you couldn't see yourself moving forward without them? Regardless of where you went and who you spoke to, the yearning inside wouldn't let you rest. Your effort to reach out was fueled by how much this person means to you. Feeling astoundingly hurt at the possibility that they might not come back, you had to let go until they returned. Even as this seemed like it was the only option, there was a hum that you just couldn't ignore. It mingled with the deep longing, pulsing in your soul that one day the person you love would come back.

Relationships as they are, serve a great purpose in your life, and when something happens to severe the connection it creates a void. Other things, like blurred misunderstandings, can come in to keep you apart,

Our relationship with Jesus (Yahwey) can often resemble the taters and fragments of a broken relationship. For the children of Israel, they found themselves in captivity, and spiritually separated from God, because of their outright disobedience. The relationship was no longer at the place where it should have been as in time past. Yet there was still a shred of hope.

Through the prophet Jeremiah, the Lord sent a message to His people saying, *"Then shall ye call upon me, and ye shall go and pray unto me, and I will hearken unto you. And ye shall seek me, and find me, when ye shall search for me with all your heart"* (Jeremiah 29:12-13).

Such words signified that while anger ruminated in God, He still wanted the children of Israel to seek for Him. The thoughts He had towards them were of *"peace and not of evil and to give [them] a future and a hope."* (Jeremiah 29:11[NKJV])

In the book of Isaiah, the same choice is given to God's people, *"… Seek ye the Lord while he may be found, [and to] call ye upon him while he is near"* (Isaiah 55:6).

While it is an invitation of opportunity to seek, it also stipulates an underling warning of *"while he may be found…and while he is near"*

When you seek God, it means you are communicating with Him. You are consistently, *"spending time in His presence"* and learning who He is. While certain behaviours, and bad choices, leads to a breakup, and it can be challenging to admit where you have gone wrong. Whatever the case might be, there is still an opportunity to make it right. Even if you feel so guilty you can't summon the strength to even make an attempt, to reach out, Wisdom professes *"I love them that love me; and those that seek me early shall find me"* (Proverbs 8:17).

While there is time, and life is circulating through your veins, Jesus is waiting for you to open your heart to Him. You do not have to allow shame and guilt to rob you of your chance to have a relationship with your Creator.

Seek ye the Lord.
Call ye upon Him.
Near, near He is
and this You must achieve.

TODAY, YOU CAN SING THE LORD'S SONG:
"LORD IF YOU HEAR MY CRY AND WHILE I DO
HAVE THE TIME LET ME FIND YOU"

Scripture Reference
Isaiah 55:6 ◆ Proverbs 8:17 ◆ Jeremiah 29:12-13

Your Day's Reflection

_____

_____

_____

_____

_____

_____

_____

Nobody but Jesus

Among the gods there is none like unto thee, O Lord;
neither are there any works like unto thy works.
♦ *Psalms 86:8*

Neither is there salvation in any other: for there is none other name
under heaven given among men, whereby we must be saved.
♦ *Acts 4:12*

THE VERSE

Under the heavens, in the earth,
and the entire universe, there is none like Thee.
From Your hands, You cradle life,
from Your worthiness, You open seals.

No deity can walk the line of sacrifice
or carry the cross upon which You bleed.
Nobody gives man hope for a life without conditions.
In order to reclaim self-fish intentions.

All around, all around we search
and there is no one like Thee.

Your Name is precious with swords,
blazing with rage to cut imitating divinities.

Your name is sung on the lips of children,
who are innocent from the truth.
With unfailing conviction, they decorate
Your name with melody and harmony
Little they are, but they know there is none like Thee.

With life at the tip,
my faith rests upon whom You conquered.
This I can sing, this I can say,
In my life, You must stay.
In my world, You are Lord.

How can I walk away and never remember?
How can I see that there are others better than Thee?
Who can be born of a woman and remain loyal?
Come from the seed to bruise serpent heads?

Who can crack the sky like thunder?
Break the cedars of Lebanon?

Who can be the friend to contain secrets,
even when dispelled, walk away and keep them?

Who can make us walk on the sea of the earth?
Who can drown and defeat our hungry enemies?

Who can hold the body
when it wanes amidst the pangs of mortality;
anchor the soul and carry it to the gates of eternity?

Who can I depend and call?
Who will give grace with everlasting mercy;
a salvation without cost?
Who will write the names of saints in the book of life?
Who will understand tears when the heart is
contorted and twisted with groanings?

Who will save and embrace us after we have fallen?

Whose name can we call in despair?
Whose name can we sing in praise?
Whose name can we wear after birth?

Nobody, Nobody but Jesus
Nobody, nobody but You can enter the heart
and make it well.
Nobody, nobody can enter the veil and rent in two.
Nobody, nobody can pay my redemptions dues.
Nobody, nobody but You

YOUR SONG

Nobody but Jesus.
Nobody but my Saviour
No one else
Cause He's done so much for me
And there is no way that I would ever change my mind (mind)

Nobody but Jesus
Nobody but my Saviour
No one else
Cause He gives me so much joy
And there is no way that His love will ever change

Reflection

I Will Sing nobody, nobody but Jesus
He's the kind of friend I can depend on

A dime a dozen, some friends are simply irreplaceable. The bond you share is like a hidden ruby amongst the multitude of faces and sands. Once you discover such a friend, you never want to let them go. No matter how far you search through the millions of faces in the world, no one can compare to the value, treasure, joy and happiness this friend brings to your life. From past experiences of the good and bad times, you can count on the possibility they will always be there for you. If the need arises, you know they will be more than willing to make a sacrifice, even if it takes more from them than from you. Between friends and or family, this particular person could be anyone, and if your heart is ready, you will cherish that bond forever for as long as you live.

Do you have a friend whom you know that you can depend? It is a friend who will stay with you everywhere you go. Who can compare to such a friend?

From the wonders, and experience of God's Magnificent power, Moses asks this question.

"Who is like You, O Lord, among the gods? Who is like You, glorious in holiness, Fearful in praises, doing wonders?" (Exodus 15:11)

From the splendor of God's love in the form of Jesus, He became that sacrifice. He performed many miracles, raising the dead, and healing the sick. He baffled those who followed and were more curious about whether or not he was for real.

During a terrible storm, and watching Jesus rebuke it, those who were in the boat with him asked, *"…What kind of man is this, that even the winds and sea obey him?"* (Mattityahu (Mat) 8:27b [CJB])

***"Greater love hath no man than this, that a man lay down his life for his friends."* (John 15:13)**

When you think about what God can do, and the miracles manifested through Jesus, it begs the question: *who will lay down their life? Who will give up the breath in their body for a friend?* Who would be worthy enough to die in the manner Jesus did, for an entire human race. When only a percentage of that race will accept, cherish and honor that sacrifice? Then there are the questions of who will perform the healing of miracles when you are sick?

Without a doubt, there are incidents of friends, and family members who will go to great extent to show you how much they love can care. *They are those* who will commit themselves to causes for a greater purpose than for personal benefits. On the other hand, while they may consider the cost, it still does not stop them from backing out.

But for the kind of love Jesus gives, it is next to impossible to find. As you live and breathe, even in the afterlife of eternity- in Christ - Jehovah continues to do the impossible for which you could never even dream. When human effort fails, Jesus is that friend upon which you can depend.

The Apostle Peter rightfully puts it like this, *"Neither is there salvation in any other: for there is none other name under heaven given among men, whereby we must be saved."* (Acts 4:12)

Reflecting on your own life, you can even ask the question: Who has been there to pick you up when all else has failed. Who provided the roof over your head when others have closed the door on you?

Whose name can [you] call in despair?
Whose name can [you] sing in praise?
Whose name can [you] wear after birth?

Nobody, Nobody but Jesus
Nobody, Nobody but Emmanuel

Today, you can sing the Lord's song "Nobody, Nobody but Jesus"

Scripture Reference
Psalms 86:8 ♦ Exodus 14:11; 15:11 ♦ Acts 4:12 ♦ John 15: 13-14

Your Day's Reflection

_____

_____

_____

_____

_____

_____

_____

_____

Whom do You say that I'AM?

He saith unto them, But whom say ye that I am. ◆ **Matthew 16:15**

I am Alpha and Omega, the beginning and the end,
the first and the last ◆ **Revelation 22:13**

THE VERSE

There is a truth,
There is a lie,
There is a song,
There is a hand holding on.

There are eyes seeing,
There are stories gleaming,
There is a time,
There is a word.
A collective of language,
about who I AM.

Clapping palms catch the opportunity to praise and worship.
Clapping children, mothers, fathers, sisters' brothers, pastors, saints,
believers, non-believers, experience, rejoicing celebrating
who I am.

I tell you this, because you should know

---

there is a wing that drives into the channel;
to kidnap the seed not yet planted about who I AM

But this I must ask of thee
Do you know who I AM?
Do you understand who I AM?
Do you believe who I AM?
Do you see who I AM?

Can you listen to the I AM?
Can you hear the I AM?

My voice *is* a thread holding the confidence
sown in the hearts of true men.
Like a light in the uncomprehensive darkness, it reveals the mess.
It showcases honesty,
it holds princes and princesses,
molded from royalty.

Many talk and say a lot about who I AM?
But I must ask of thee, whom say ye that I AM?

YOUR SONG

You are our Father, our creator
The one in the beginning, The Word,
You are Almighty, and there is no other

You are God, and You are I AM
You are God the GREAT I AM

You are our healer, Our Provider
You're the God of righteousness and truth
You are our comfort, and You are our keeper

You are God, and You are I AM
You are God the Great I AM

You are the Bread of life, our hope and salvation
You are the way, the truth, and the life
You're the Alpha and Omega, and You are Lord above all
You are Jesus, and You are I AM
You are Jesus the GREAT I AM
You are God, and you are I am
You are Jesus the GREAT I AM

Reflection

There is a significant difference between knowing someone versus having a general idea about who they are. For example: amongst you and your family, no one has to give you a hint about what you already know. If someone were to tell you your parents' names were Jeff and Susan, *different from what you know*, it would be impossible for you to believe because you know your parents. Just like your parents know you. You'd be more inclined to correct the "supposed" mistake than to accept otherwise. This is because of the length of time you have grown to know your parents. From their name, to their personality, attitude, physical features and the sound of their voice, you would not second guess yourself. If you were asked to describe or even point them out in a crowd, you would hardly struggle. Imagine how you would feel if the person who should know you the most does not know your name. Especially after spending so much time with them? *Have you ever asked your loved ones the question, "Do you know who I am?"*

For any type of relation, it is important to consider how you are influenced by what others tell you, about your loved ones. Perhaps, there is someone you are considering to be your friend and or spouse. Is your perception of them based on what others tell you?

Given how and why Jesus came, countless opinions were ruminating in the minds of the people who followed Him. Out of all the miracles He performed and the number of things He said, the disciples were the ones who would've have had a better understanding of the man who raised the dead.

One day while conversing with the disciples, He asked a poignant question:

"Who do men say that I, the Son of Man, AM?"

They replied saying, "Some say John the Baptist, some Elijah, and others Jeremiah or one of the prophets."

Jesus countered saying, *"But who do you say that I am?"*

Simon Peter, who was close to Jesus, and one of the twelve disciples, replied, saying,

"You are the Christ, the Son of the living God."

Such a response warranted Jesus to tell Peter:

> *"Blessed are you, Simon Bar-Jonah, for flesh and blood has not revealed this to you, but My Father who is in heaven. And I also say to you that you are Peter, and on this rock, I will build My church, and the gates of [hell] shall not prevail against it. And I will give you the keys of the kingdom of heaven, and whatever you bind on earth will be bound in heaven, and whatever you loose on earth will be loosed in heaven"* (Matthew 16:13-19 ᴺᴷᴶⱽ).

In comparison to what many others believed and said, the question Jesus asked, surely brought to the forefront, the belief of the disciples. Depending on their response, it would reveal how much they knew. Or it would show how the opinions of others influenced what they believed to be true. Based on how Peter answered however, Jesus proclaimed that Peter would be the one upon which the church would be built.

Based on what you know about Jesus, do you believe what others are telling you about Him? Are you willing to get to know Him for yourself? Are you ready to seek Him for yourself? If you are struggling in your faith and not feeling secure, the Lord will send a Word whether through a song or scriptural verse to encourage and affirm about who He is.

There is a truth about who I am.
There is a lie about who I am.
There is a song of who I am.
There is a hand holding who I am.

Tᴏᴅᴀʏ, ʏᴏᴜ ᴄᴀɴ sɪɴɢ ᴛʜᴇ Lᴏʀᴅ's sᴏɴɢ "Yᴏᴜ
ᴀʀᴇ Gᴏᴅ ᴛʜᴇ **GREAT I AM**"

Scripture Reference
Matthew 16:13-19 ♦ Exodus 3:14 ♦ Revelation 22:13

Your Day's Reflection

_____

_____

_____

_____

_____

_____

_____

_____

_____

When You Speak

The voice of the Lord is upon the waters: the God of glory thundereth:
the Lord is upon many waters. The voice of the Lord is powerful;
the voice of the Lord is full of majesty. ♦ **Psalms 29:4-3**

…My sheep hear my voice, and I know them, and
they follow me ♦ **John 10:27** NKJV

THE VERSE

The quality of Your voice sets the stage,
and I am ready to stand and listen,
so that I can walk the way You have ordained.

Other voices do speak for matters,
giving perfect solutions for problems altogether.
With my uncertainties I climb the steps to Your throne.

Sifting through the opinions,
I examine the unknowns and qualities.
My assumptions bridge acceptance,
but this factor is critical to my existence.
I need to hear,
I need to know,
when You speak.

For it is Your voice,
the string-pulling broken fragments back to together.

Therefore, I cannot abide under the shadows of flawed intelligence.
Added together it will not quantify for peace.

From Your mouth, the words of life spring forth from the seed planted.

The waters recognize Your wisdom,
and they cannot surpass nor remain on the shores of men.

Bountiful of life it is to speak of your splendor, nonetheless it must obey.

In seasons it gives and takes.
The process is an order:
Increase and multiply.
Grow up the trees.
Mist the space as we breathe.

When my pain consumes me so,
it comes with the dialogue,
where do I go?
Who do I listen to?

I need to hear. I need to know,
when You speak.

Those who do speak Your mind are appointed and anointed
with rich solutions.
It cascades from their gown;
jewels so cherished the price is too much to count.

Some voices validate.
Wrong or right, some voices mock.
Speak lies telling stories seemingly from on high.
Wrong or right,

how do I choose?

The sheep, I am, humility is the value.
If they feed my mouth, it is possible to eat.
If they lead me on it is possible to follow.

Even in this,
God upon waters,
voice of the mysteries
I need to know.
I need to hear when You speak.

YOUR SONG

I go to the Word for answers
and search the scripture to find
Seek him while He can be found
I have learned I need to build that relationship and then I will know
I will know Your voice.

I want to know Your voice
I want to know when You speak
I need to hear You very clear
I want to know when You speak
There is nothing else that matters in this world,
if I cannot know when You speak

Reflection

Virtually most mothers and fathers instinctively know their children's voice, and visa-versa. Through the variable stages of human growth, a nurtured child develops a deep connection with their parents. This bond and intern signal guides the child to know when their parents are talking to them. Between strange and familiar voices the child more than likely will be able to discern the differences. It will also determine if the child can resist certain kinds of council contrary to what their parents have taught them. When someone you know calls out to you, instinctively, you can pick up the wavelength, texture, and tone of their voice. The sound you hear is familiar, and you are less confused than if it is someone you do not know.

Do you know the voices calling out to you?

As child of God, you are born into the faith by baptism and in-filling of the Holy-Spirit. By taking on the Name of Jesus, you become His child. Before and after birth, you have already established a connection. Your spirit is intuitively attracted to the voice of Jesus when He calls your name.
While talking to the Pharisees, Jesus said,

> *"To him the doorkeeper opens, and the sheep hear his voice; and he calls his own sheep by name and leads them out. And when he brings out his own sheep, he goes before them; and the sheep follow him, for they know his voice. Yet they will by no means follow a stranger, but will flee from him, for they do not know the voice of strangers." (John 10:3-5 ESV).*

As simple and clear as that sounds, the Pharisees still didn't understand, so Jesus spoke again, *"…Truly, truly, I say to you, I am the door of the sheep. All who came before me are thieves and robbers, but the sheep did not listen to them" (John 10: 7-8).*

While this would've helped, there was unbelief, and a group of them believed Jesus had a devil. During the Feast of Dedication in Jerusalem, a group came to Jesus, asking him again to explain in simple terms if He was the Christ. Answering them, He said, *"...I told you, and you do not believe. The works that I do in My Father's name, they bear witness of Me. But you do not believe, because you are not of My sheep, as I said to you. My sheep hear My voice, and I know them, and they follow Me."* (John 10:25-27 ESV).

Not mincing His words, Jesus told them the truth, and of course, they wanted to stone Him. As he pointed out and explained, there are voices which might sound the same, but they are distinct. If you find yourself confused about a particular situation, it is best to talk to your Heavenly Father for counsel. But most importantly, know it is Him talking back.

In the natural order of things, sheep are known for having the capability to remember faces and voices. They will not follow a stranger's voice. For Jesus sheep, there are so many voices out there that do call. Some are familiar, strange, unique, and downright deceptive. Jesus' voice can get embedded in the noise of situations as well as your voice. This can lead to confusion where you can become perplexed about what to do. But if you do *"know"* Him who calls you, and if you are sensitive enough, you'll hear and listen. You will discern the difference between what God and others say. Even if it takes time for you to know or hear a voice in a crowd, when you *"seek"* to spend time with God, like a friend or relative, over time, the voice will stand out to you.

Sifting through the opinions,
[you] can examine the unknowns and qualities.
but this factor is critical to your existence.
You need to hear,
You need to know,
when [He] speaks

TODAY YOU CAN SING THE LORD'S SONG " I WILL KNOW YOUR VOICE."

Scripture Reference
Psalms 29:4-3 ♦ John 10:3-5; 7-8a; 25-27

Your Day's Reflection

_____

_____

_____

_____

_____

_____

_____

_____

_____

I Want to Sing Your Song

Let Your Word Abide in Me

But he answered and said, It is written, Man shall not live by bread alone, but by every word that proceedeth out of the mouth of God. ♦ **Matthew 4:3** NKJV

Heaven and earth shall pass away, but my words shall not pass away. ♦ **Matthew 24:35**

THE VERSE

Sitting on the throne of my heart is Your word.
I know I cannot forget it.

In the way towards promise and glory,
the choice is there to walk away
or keep on living the called-out life.

In my freedom to choose, I contend.
Between spirit and flesh,
both are hungry, and both should eat.

Deep down, the spirit and soul sing a song.
In the vine of righteousness, I am fed.
Let Your word, let Your word abide in me

The savory taste of survival is good on the tongue.

Towards the prize of satisfaction, I pursue priorities and success.
Yet in time I'm reminded that food is not enough.
It cannot sustain for the times of brokenness.

At midnight, curtains hide the pain.
At sunrise, the tears reveal none of the same.
The people I love may comfort,
but at the closing of days, all I have is Your promise.

When I might lose treasures that bring joy, it is easy to cave in
and collapse into the trenches where no man can find me.

It is easy to let go and let the fowls of the air have their way.

When I don't know how to love You, teach me the fruit of longsuffering.

When I lose my way in the forest of voices howling like wolves to moons,
words of salvation anchor my soul.
Abide in me Word of truth,
Abide in me Word of belief.

In the ground, the tree is rooted.
The storm clouds arise, and the test comes.

My heart might break, and my soul groans for comfort.
Yet, it is Your Word I reach for; a companion in places of slumber.

As the earth does change colors, and the
people I know have come and gone,
the lights turn out, and the city sleeps.
A peace I don't understand settles the score of storms.
On my own, I am refreshed by the telling of Your strength and power.

In the wake of uncertainty, I coddle the precious
Living Bread; I dare not let it go.

Word of God.
Word of Truth.
Let this Word abide in me
For I shall not live by bread alone

YOUR SONG

I shall not live by bread alone, but by every word
that proceedeth out Your mouth.
Day by day and every morning, God's Word is true
Your Word must abide in me
And I must abide in Your Word
Night by night I pray
Let your word, let word abide in me

Let Your Word (*Let Your Word*)
Let Your Word (*Let Your Word*)
Let Your Word, Let Your Word abide in me

Reflection

Words which are a part of the human dialect, and culture, serve a great purpose for expression. Formed into language and a diversity of context, it is just as essential as being able to recognize a voice. For the things you will say to people and how you say it is significant because words express the things that you need to hear. As you will develop into the person you are meant to be, food is not the only nourishment your parents will provide for you. They will give you a word to keep you anchored in the way you ought to grow. Their words will guide you on how to deal with problems when they arise. As you go along, while you might forget most of what they said, you will remember the key things they would've told you.

Words of sound wisdom are treasures to be cherished.

After fasting for 40 days and 40 nights, Jesus, being led by the Spirit, walked into the wilderness. It was a place not suitable for any human to find food to eat. While Jesus was there, the "tempter" being none other than the devil, came and said,

"If you are the Son of God, command that these stones become bread" (Matthew 4:3 AMP)

With whatever strength Jesus had, he replied and said, *"It is written, Man shall not live by bread alone, but by every word that proceedeth out of the mouth of God."*

While this should've ended the conversation, the devil took Jesus up into the holy city. set Him on the pinnacle of the temple, and said to Him,

"If you are the Son of God throw Yourself down. For it is written 'He shall give His angels charge over you, and, In their hands they shall bear you up, Lest you dash your foot against a stone.'"

The devil was not letting up as he jeered Jesus to test the laws of gravity as well as His pride! But countering with the same word, Jesus replied,

I Want to Sing Your Song

"It is written again, You shall not tempt the Lord your God."

The devil then got bolder. He brought Jesus to an *"exceedingly"* high mountain and showed Him all the kingdoms of the world. "All these things I will give You if You will fall down and worship me."

Jesus surely had enough, *"Away with you, Satan! For it is written, 'You shall worship the Lord your God, and Him only you shall serve."* (Matthew 4:8-11)

Such tactics are no different than what you will face when the enemy of your soul engages you to sin. It is important to understand that even though Jesus used the word – *three times* - the devil was not giving up his intentions to get Jesus to succumb to his flesh. What is even more disconcerting is how the devil used the same word to tempt Jesus. He also took it as far as to tell Jesus to worship him.

While the devil is evil, he is not the only enemy you have to deal with.

When you are born, the nature of sin is already there. Paul, who had his struggles, acknowledged the factors of good and evil being present:

"For I know that in me (that is, in my flesh) nothing good dwells; for to will is present with me, but how to perform what is good I do not find. For the good that I will to do, I do not do; but the evil I will not to do, that I practice." (Romans 7:18-19)

As this is disconcerting and we do struggle as Jesus demonstrated, it is with the Word of God that you overcome. Like the words of your mother or father, the Word is your strength in times of temptation, trials and tribulation. It is also written: *"...resist the devil and he will flee from you."* (James 4:7b) When you are confronted by the devil and his deceptive conversations, the Word abiding in you will be your weapon to ward him off. Not only that it will keep you anchored as you go along

In the wake of uncertainty, ... coddle the precious
Living Bread; ... dare not let it go.

Let this Word abide in [you]
For [you] shall not live by bread alone

Today You can sing the Lord's song, "I shall not live by bread alone, but by every word that proceedeth out your mouth"

Scripture Reference
Matthew 4:4;6 ♦ John 15:7 ♦ Matthew 24
♦ 1 Corinthians 14:15 ♦ James 4:7

Your Day's Reflection

_____

_____

_____

_____

_____

_____

_____

_____

_____

Formed in Reverence

For thou hast possessed my reins: thou hast covered me in my mother's womb. I will praise thee; for I am fearfully and wonderfully made: marvelous are thy works; and that my soul knoweth right well. ♦ **Psalms 139:13-14**

The Verse

With the story like a puzzle,
ready to be written,
in the shadows of Your concept my life was given.

When I had no thought of myself,
nor could make the choice to live,
You shaped my bones and molded the quality of who I am to be.

Sinew to Sinew.
Breath to breath.
Reason sanctioned,
Let us, let us make this image.
Let us, let us make this decision.

Possessed in Your hands,
You held my soul in the palms of Your domain.

From the expansive fields of creation
to the wholesome sea,

beauty was made perfect.

At the tip of Your touch,
I became Your purpose.

Your vision, no angel could see, despite the flaw,
You still gave the world a wonder to see.

Like the morning of harmonious songs
You are the archetype for which I was to be and is.

Marvelous are Thy works
What a wonder,
What a reverence,
Such tenderness,
My soul needs to know this for the past and present.

I may become dirty
and sometimes unworthy.
Nonetheless dignity is my friend
and the story is Yours to commend.

You shaped the hands to possess power
You placed the feet to walk the line of dreams.
You gave the heart to pant after purpose.
You gave the ears to hear timeless assurance.
You gave the eyes to see endless days
and gave me the will to exist in the land of wondrous ways.

Ascribed as an emblem for my mother's faith, and my father's vision,
You wrought my soul on the table of Your grace.

While I could not sound my freedom to live,
You gave the purpose to the angels
to encamp around the soul and carry me.

Holding my reins, You direct my character
to take on the attributes of Your impeccable nature.

Laid out before me is the call to get up.
To arise from the slumber of invisibility,
to arise and tear down the walls of hiding the light.

Wherever I go people must know,
others must see
It's okay to breathe

Whispers will come to nimble at the heel
It will give the flawed truth that I do not matter.

But no matter what the manipulative arguments
say, I am the designed gift
Revered in Yahweh's image.

Fearfully and wonderfully
wearing treasures glistening on my physique.
Up on the hills of Zion, I shine the light of glory.

In the city where darkness veils,
my presence is linked to others not to be hid.

What a wonder
What a promise
What a freedom
No shame
No guilt
This is my revered body.
This is my revered hands
This is my revered stance
I am Me.
No apology

YOUR SONG

What a wonder
What a reverence
In your image You made me
This is what You made (X2)
You made my eyes and my feet
You have me my voice so I can shout and sing
This is what You made (X2)

Oh how precious
Are Your thoughts
Like the sand and the stars
You possess my rein
You possess soul
This is what you made
This is what you made

Fearfully wonderfully made
In Your hands there are no mistakes.
My substance not hid from You.
Curiously wrought.
This is what You made.
This is what You made.

Reflection

Without question, beautiful, gorgeous, handsome, are words you will often hear within the context of admiral esteem for physical comeliness. At the same time, there are individual perceptions, which contrast against the idea of what is exceptionally beautiful and good enough. In the entertainment and beauty industry, this idea is emphasized by a plethora of men and women portrayed in a physical fashion. Illustrated through a category of dramatization, the image of a woman who is visibly beautiful, and a man viably handsome, influences the notion of how an individual is to think, feel and strive towards a "natural" appeal. From both sides of the spectrum, however, opinions fluctuate, and there are mindsets conditioned to accept the societal standards and concepts of what is physically attractive.

Initially, from the stages of your upbringing, the people in your life would have encouraged or discouraged you about the way you should feel about yourself. They could have said anything, and it was in those moments, the perception of how you should feel about yourself took root. Within your internal dialogue, your self-esteem, perception, and belief engage you to analyze if what they were saying is true. But what is of most significance is your own inner agency to harness the resilience to say,

"I am beautiful",

"I am handsome."

For this kind of confidence, it would derive from the knowledge, wisdom, and understanding of how you came to be.

Similar to all living things, there is a process of how you were created. Through this process, something beautiful happened. You were given life.

Recognized as a great psalmist, David expresses and acknowledges the "revered" process which God – the Creator - took to create every breathing living being.

Praising the Lord, he says, *"For thou hast possessed my reins: thou hast covered me in my mother's womb. I will praise thee; for I am fearfully and wonderfully made: marvellous are thy works; and that my soul knoweth right well. My substance was not hid from thee when I was made in secret and curiously wrought in the lowest parts of the earth …How precious also are thy thoughts unto me, O God! how great is the sum of them!"* (Psalm 139: 13-15, 17).

Connecting back to the days of creations, by ingenious (clever) creativity, God started moving across the face of the deep. He called forth the substance and creatures of the earth. But what is quite interesting and remarkable is how He says, *"Let the earth bring forth the living creature after his kind, cattle, and creeping thing, and beast of the earth after his kind…"*

Then on the sixth day of creation, He said *"Let us make man in our image, after our likeness…"* (Gen 1:25-26a)

Similar to how He said, "after their kind" for the living creatures, for mankind He said, "after our likeness."

It might be challenging to fathom, but the Creator "multiplied" Himself. Some would argue and say, "there is no living being like God", but the word "likeness" is referred to something that is replicated – a photocopy. So, like how the animals are to multiply after their kind, God - in essence multiplied His image and likeness after Himself in us. The word "kind" in this pronouncement also means type, character, gender, nature, temperament, race, and breed.

Therefore, even though mankind was formed from dust, the quality of a man and a woman is after God's "likeness".

"Fearfully and wonderfully made," says it all, and when you think about the process of how you came to be, you'll come to understand all parts of you (inside and out) are precious and priceless in the sight of God. No matter how society may set the standard of beauty, God by His sovereignty "possessed" your substance with "reverence," and that is how much you are worth. "No Apology"

So, when you look in the mirror, and see yourself what do you see?

What a wonder
What a promise
What a freedom
No shame
No guilt…

Today, you can look in the mirror, and sing
the lord's song "What a wonder
What a reverence
In your image You made me
This is what You made"

Scripture Reference
♦ Psalms 139: 13-18

Your Day's Reflection

_____

_____

_____

_____

_____

_____

_____

_____

_____

_____

My Body is Your Temple

For ye are bought with a price: therefore, glorify God in
your body, and in your spirit, which are God's
♦ **I Corinthians 6:20**

Mortify therefore your members which are upon the earth;
fornication, uncleanness, inordinate affection, evil concupiscence,
and covetousness, which is idolatry: ♦ ***Colossians 3:5***

THE VERSE

This is the truth I must consider.
This is the truth that I will carry to the end.

Wrought from the substance of the earth.
without question, I came to be.

Wherever I go,
Whatever I do
this is the light shining on my Heavenly Father's truth.

My body is the temple.
My body is the light.
It is what I give for a continuous sacrifice.

In the hallow places not seen,

I will therefore mortify and gratify
the contemptuous seed.

For it is not what is on the outside,
but that which is within that defiles the land.

A house without walls, the discretion cries for
vigilance and somberness to be my guide.

The spirit already knows the difference between good and evil.
Deeds measured by your grace; I must be careful by what I say.

Let the words of this mouth be pleasing in Thy sight.
Let it be done even in the cool of nights.

Let it not tamper the message.
There are some places I cannot go.
Some songs I should not hear.
Some songs I cannot sing.

In the pools of Your words, and by way of consecration, I am cleansed.

There is much to measure from the abundance of days gone.
For the heart marinates in seasons long gone.
It can imprison the past away and yet to come.

But on the altar of precision,
for healing and deliverance
I therefore mortify this flesh
and resurrect the living spirit.

This is the truth I consider.
This is the truth I accept.
My body is the temple.
My body is the vessel.
This is where You come and dwell.

Your Song

My Body is the temple
My body is the temple
My body is the temple of the living God (it is)
My body is the house
My body is the house
My body is the house of the living God

So let me walk right before you
Let me talk right before you
I let me live right before you
My living God

I'll glorify you Lord, in my body and Spirit
This is the vessel, this is the place
This is where you come and dwell

Reflection

While it is key to understand that you are fearfully and wonderfully made, it is equally central to knowing who you are. It will determine how you will choose to carry and conduct yourself both privately and publicly.

One day, while you are in the company of friends, you are engaged in a series of casual laughter and chatter. The conversation steers through various subjects before it lands on a specific name of the person you know. It is your good friend, whom you have known for a long time. As the conversation progresses, certain things are revealed, which do not necessarily shed a positive light on the person being discussed.

At this point, a lot is going on in your mind, and your conscious is already kicked into gear. You are presented with a few options to take: [1] Stop the conversation the moment the name drops. [2] Remain silent while you listen and wait to see how far this will go. [3] Or express your displeasure while leaving the room.

As the differing options come before you, you begin to feel the stark difference between who you are and the depth to which this conversation will take you. For what is said, you weigh your actions and see if it's something worth doing. Your inner "option" activates *engage or disengage*.

**The quality and nature of who you are also rests
on how you choose to behave and treat yourself,
for God gave you freewill and willpower.**

Paul, a man of great exploits, wrote letters with subject matters that addressed and confronted certain behaviours in the church. In one of the letters to Corinth, he asked a reflective but also poignant question *"What? know ye not that your body is the temple of the Holy Ghost which is in you, which ye have of God, and ye are not your own?"* He went further on to say.

"For ye are bought with a price: therefore, glorify God in your body, and in your spirit, which are God's." (1 Corinthians 6:19-20).

In context, Paul was confronting lewd behaviour, but at the same time, the principle of his words underlines the quality of the human body. It is not just of carnal nature, but it does house the mind, heart, spirit, and soul.

The soul, which is the organic nature of mankind, originates from the essence of God. Through redemption, once you take on the name of Jesus, your body becomes the sacred place for the living God. Wherever you are, the Holy Spirit dwells within, and since this is an invisible entity, your body also becomes the physical representation of Christ. Which is why Paul encourages the church to "Mortify...your members...." (Colossians 3:5a)

In words or deed, whatever you decide to do, it is crucial to understand, your choice of action can be a reflection on your character as well your family and those connected to you. While reputation is an area to consider, it is even more vital to acknowledge how your choice of behaviour can have a long-lasting effect on you internally. It is a sounding belief that *"What makes a person unclean is not what goes into his mouth; rather, what comes out of his mouth, that is what makes him unclean!"* (Mattityahu (Mat) 15:11 CJB).

**For all matters of life, how you choose to conduct yourself
and treat your body as well as other people, matters.**

Wherever [you] *go.*
Whatever [you] *do, this is the light shining on*
[your] *Heavenly Father's truth.*

TODAY, YOU CAN SING THE LORD'S SONG RIGHT "THIS IS THE VESSEL.
THIS IS THE PLACE. THIS IS WHERE YOU COME AND DWELL"

Scripture Reference
1 Corinthians 6:20 ♦ Colossians 3:5 ♦ Matthew 15:11

I Want to Sing Your Song

Your Day's Reflection

_____

_____

_____

_____

_____

_____

_____

_____

_____

Renewed in the Spirit of My Mind

And be renewed in the spirit of your mind ♦ **Ephesians 4:23**

Casting down imaginations, and every high thing that exalteth itself against the knowledge of God, and bringing into captivity every thought to the obedience of Christ;
♦ **2 Corinthians 10:5**

Let this mind be in you, which was also in Christ Jesus ♦ **Philippians 2:5**

THE VERSE

Oh Lord, oh Lord
In the mind, amidst the billows of a thrilling storm,
the fragments of that which had happened,
roam through the castle spaces of the imagination.

It roams and mingles, creating the thought of what I shall do.
While the heart wrestles for charity
Let my mind settle on whatever so ever things are true.

Let my mind concentrate on that which is
honest and on that which is just.
Oh Lord, Keeper of thoughts

Let me keep my mind on praise and virtue.

Keeper of the soul, the prince of peace.
Walk with me to unending days; help me not to lose my way.

Ruminating in the pool of foresight,
I see the reflection of my soul, caught between the new and the old.

In the way, the rise of actions leaves breadcrumbs
upon the trail, which leads to Canaan.

In the wake of contemplation,
the storms of memory song chime the choice.
Will I make it?
Will I dance?
Will I Survive?
Will all there is to be of me last?

This is a need to be addressed by Your Word
that it enriching and nutritious.

My mind consistently yearns for the renewal.
What I think see and do,
the inner man is convinced of what to do.

Fitly joined, it is with wholesomeness,
I can see beyond what seemingly is to be.
I reason the differences between disparity.

Whether good or evil, it is there.
But this I know and cling to.

Casting down and lifting,
may the Word like a double-edge sword,
stand guard at the gate.

Of righteousness and song,
let it cut down the thoughts of that which is wrong.

The God who is always there.
Renew my mind when it runs from devotion.
Renew my mind when it is compromised.

Renew my mind when it sees too much.
Renew my mind when seeds of decay have been planted.

Renew my mind when I'm lost in the vaults of discourse.

Renew my mind, so I'll always think of Your holy courts.

With my head lifted and my heart beating, let this mind be like Christ.
Let this mind think to do that, which is wise.
Let this mind renew daily from the coming and goings.
Let it remember all that You taught me, so I know where I'm going.

For whatsoever things are lovely, it is on these things I shall think.

YOUR SONG

Lord, it's with my mind I serve You
May my thoughts be pure and true
Be a living sacrifice, Holy and acceptable unto you
And as I meditate on Your Word
I want to be transformed from within,
to bare the fruits of Your sweet Spirit
This is my humble prayer

Let me keep my mind on
Whatever is true and honest
Whatever is just and pure
Whatever is holy and of good report
of virtue and of praise

Reflection

There is absolutely nothing in this world that is more treasurable, fragile, and precious than the complete health of a wholesome mind. As a continuous meditative practice, taking care of the mind is essential to survival. Central to the entire body, it is undoubtedly powerful. Under normal circumstances, it can be challenged by ideas, concepts, and theories of life. From series of events and experiences, how you process such occurrences depends upon your inner agency. Concerning how the mind can be renewed, diverse fields of study have presented and demonstrated research to support the theory of mindfulness. According to the study of Michelle Mars and Oliver Megan "With regular practice, mindfulness is a powerful tool that can help you improve your overall wellbeing" [1] Generally speaking the main concern rests on the sense of awareness, being present, and in being in the moment. As Mars and Meegan explain "...It's letting go of past regrets and the worries of what the future might bring." [2]

There are numbers of books out there that talk about the health of the mind. But from the Word of Life, there are scriptures which address how and why you should take care of it.

During his time in Ephesus, Paul exhorted, saying,
"That ye put off concerning the former conversation the old man, which is corrupt according to the deceitful lusts; And be renewed in the spirit of your mind..." (Ephesians 4:22-24)

In observance of the word, *"renewed"*, it is fundamentally a state of being. It is being re-established. It is being repaired, recovered, and revived. As it is connected to your spirit and the rest of your being, your mind plays a vital role in how your body, heart, and spirit function from day to day. Affiliated with the mind your heart it is just as precious and even more vulnerable. Of King Solomon's proverb, it is written saying, *"Keep thy heart with all diligence; for out of it are the issues of life"* (Proverb 4:23)

With your mind, it processes the information that you receive through your ear, and eye gate. Interconnected to the heart, whatever you hear, see, touch and even say impacts how you will cope with conflicts as they come. Of a truth there are "issues of life" that can disrupt your inner peace and lead you to do things you might not want to do. You could be anxious, perplex and distress, and such feelings can generate thoughts that Jesus does not care or love you. However, the antidote to effective renewal comes through this positive incentive *"…whatsoever things are true … honest, … just, … pure, … lovely, … are of good report; if there be any virtue, and if there be any praise, think on these things"* (Philippians 4:8b).

When you practice on a consistent basis to feed your mind with the Word of God, it will lead you to having a healthy lifestyle. It will help you to filter out the thoughts that are there to weaken your walk with Christ. When you center your mind on Jesus, He will be the greatest meditative antidote to keep your mind in "perfect peace..." (Isaiah 26:3a).

What I think see and do,
the inner man is convinced of what to do.

TODAY, YOU CAN SING THE LORD'S SONG OF A
RENEWED MIND "WHATEVER IS JUST AND PURE
WHATEVER IS HOLY AND OF GOOD REPORT
OF VIRTUE AND OF PRAISE"

Scripture Reference
**1 Corinthians 6:20 ♦ Romans 12:1 ♦ Colossians
3:5 ♦ Matthew 15:11 ♦ Isaiah 26:3**

I Want to Sing Your Song

Your Day's Reflection

_____

_____

_____

_____

_____

_____

_____

_____

_____

_____

The Walk of Thy Statutes

Therefore, thou shalt love the Lord thy God, and keep his charge, and his statutes, and his judgments, and his commandments, always ♦ **Deuteronomy 11:1**

For all the law is fulfilled in one word, even in this; Thou shalt love thy neighbour as thyself.
♦ **Galatians 5:14**

THE VERSE

The laws of Your word have mapped the steps
for my spirit, and mind to take.
On the pilgrim journey toward the New Jerusalem,
the leading of Your staff supports the weight of my body.
It supports the hands to remain balanced.
It supports the feet to keep on moving.

According to the statutes of Thy Word,
there is a law for which I align myself to be Holy.
Walking in the vocation, this is the way made straight.
It is for this I shall love
I shall give
I shall let go of the weight so that I can walk upright.

At the helm of grace,

at the length of mercy,
at the leading of your staff,
at your gracious command
Let my will, aligns with Yours.

Far and wide like the sea are Your ways.
I may question things You say
Even lament Your reasons out of my reach.

But let my heart say the prayers, that are
dancing on my forefather's seat.
All in all the greatest of laws is to love.

It is to walk in the fields where hands can be joined,
and the journey is taken not alone.

The greatest of works and traditions is to edify.
The greatest of judgments is to forgive.
Speaking the fulfilled law,
it is the greatest of words.
I am to be the salt of the earth.

To be the strength for the weary,
and to be the courage for the faint in heart.

The compassion and kindness You bestow,
is the given secret of Your expression.
You don't just love one, You Jesus love the world.

While I love my neighbors as myself,
I must remember it's not just for myself.
We are all made the same, different colors of Your divine race.

Pure and holy, You have called.
In this life, on my way, I must walk,
fulfilled and satisfied is this law.

Love is right.
Love is to fight.
A tree living by waters
I flourish with the fruits,
according to Thy statutes.

YOUR SONG

At the helm of your grace
at the length of Your mercy
At the leading of Your staff
Lord I will obey

The instructions of Your Word,
At Your command
what I understand
Lord I will obey

Yahweh I will obey
Yahweh I will listen
Yahweh, I want to walk, walk in Your statutes

I must walk in, I must walk in Your statutes
I must walk in, I must walk in Your statutes

Reflection

Lifestyle, which is interconnected to your overall wellbeing and health, is in simple terms, a way of living. Beneficial to your mental, emotional, physical, and spiritual health, there are certain customs and practices that contribute to how you develop as a person. Like a circle, the social agencies of your development, influence, how you perceive, interpret, and engage the world in which you live. Categorized into your family, academics, religion, and political practices, these areas influence what you believe and understand about life. Culture, which is rooted in human traditions and practices, is a custom that generates personal and impersonal values. Certain beliefs are established, which allows for individuals and groups of people to develop strength from defaulting into what they are not. For example: with pop culture, some trends seem like they are the right thing to do because of how current and hip it is. Music that is associated with pop culture does have a significant impact on how people interpret the world and interact with one another. Because of "freedom of speech," certain lifestyles can be developed based on what is expressed or reiterated in a song. However, its impact comes down to how you are enabled to make a decision, to either adhere to or abstain. In communities of the world, some laws govern and regulate the universal lifestyle of society. For those who drive and travel by different means of transportation, this would translate to: The red light means stop!

In God's kingdom, there are spiritual statues that serve a higher purpose for your spiritual lifestyle.

After God had delivered the children of Israel out of Egypt through Moses, He gave them the Ten Commandments. Precise, clear, and specific, it emphasized how the children of Israel were to live their lives in relation to worship, and loving God. It also addressed family life, crime—marriage, neighborly, and brotherly love.

"Thou shalt have no other gods before me.... Thou shalt not kill. Thou shalt not commit adultery. Thou shalt not steal. Thou shalt not bear false witness against thy neighbor. Thou shalt not covet." (Exodus 20:3,13-17a)

A guide and light it provided them with a new way of living, according to their faith.

In the book of Galatians, it also affirmed *"For all the law is fulfilled in one word, even in this; Thou shalt love thy neighbour as thyself."* (Galatians 5:14)

In this dispensation of Grace, God's laws are not designed to counter your free will and freedom of choice. From the article of National Rationale, it is explained that

"Maintaining spiritual faithfulness according to kingdom culture is not living by a set of rules and regulations, but it is permitting the indwelling Christ to live out His life in the believer."[1] This means your faithfulness is connected to your belief system, which regulates your inner man to function according to how the Holy Spirit directs you. If He says go left, you have the choice to go the other way. However, it also means you are willing to accept what comes after you have made your choice. If it is in your heart to live the called-out life, be "renewed in your mind," and develop a healthy spiritual lifestyle, then God's statues are what you need to press forward. Similar to obeying the laws of the road, if you are to get to your destination safely, adhering to the safety signs and speed limits will determine if you will get there.

The laws of [God's] *word have mapped the steps*
for [your] *spirit, and mind to take.*
On the pilgrim journey toward the New Jerusalem,
the leading of [His] *staff supports the weight of* [Your] *body.*

TODAY, YOU CAN SING THE LORD'S SONG "AT YOUR COMMAND WHAT I UNDERSTAND LORD I WILL OBEY"

Scripture Reference
Deuteronomy 11:1♦ Proverbs 3: 1-2; 12 ♦
Matthew 22: 36-38 ♦ Matthew 5:17

I Want to Sing Your Song

Your Day's Reflection

_____

_____

_____

_____

_____

_____

_____

_____

_____

Bear Good Fruit

But the fruit of the Spirit is love, joy, peace,
longsuffering, gentleness, goodness, faith,
Meekness, temperance: against such there is no law. ◆ **Galatians 5:22-23**

For the fruit of the Spirit is in all goodness and
righteousness and truth; ◆ **Ephesians 5:9**

And he shall be like a tree planted by the rivers of water, that
bringeth forth his fruit in his season; his leaf also shall not wither;
and whatsoever he doeth shall prosper. ◆ **Psalms 1:3**

THE VERSE

Walking in Your light, I will bear fruit.
living by the rivers of waters.
By Your Spirit, I will always stand.
From my heart, I chose to love You.

By this love, men shall know I am Your child.
Against such, there is no law, no limit to how much I should give.

Love is the road that leads back home.
It leads back to the table
where hands are held with unbreakable communion.

Along the way,
there are signs and directions
on how to behave and where to go.

If I stumble and get hurt,
I can rise again, for I know there is much love for every season.

On a day when it rains and pours,
I'll extend what I have to those bruised to the core of their bones.

Nourished by the anointed joy,
always blooming in the core of peculiar times,

I maintain it well so that I may sing to the glory of the Father.

When wars and rumors come calling,
it is the peace to calm the raging suffering.

It is the peace to forgive,
it is the longsuffering to wait,
It is understanding.

Laying out the blanket to apply the gentleness,
it is the gentleness that opens the door to bring in faith.

As it enters, there is a comfort that hugs the
broken back, bended by winds.

By the countenance of a sincere smile,
the heart can operate in meekness,
and stand in temperance.

Against such, there is no law.
Against such, there is no limit.
The walk of the spirit is to be different from the call of the darkness.

It's aim is to blind the eyes, so that we can't
walk before His throne faultless.

Sometimes the fight comes to tear down that bond of great fellowship.
To divide humankind, so sin may flourish.
But from the fruit of the Spirit, rich with righteousness,
I summoned the courage to forbear and wear salvations garment.

Planted by the rivers of living waters, the leaf brings forth the good fruit.
The spirit is expounded, by what is in the mouth and consumed.
By this, all men shall know I am a child of the
King, always sitting by the Savior's feet.

Against such, there is no law.
Against such, there is no limit.
From this song, others are blessed,
from this song, others are healed.

Rivers of living waters flood my root.
In the driest of seasons, I will continue to bear good fruit.

Your Song

Walking in Your light, I will bear fruit.
Living by the rivers of waters.
By Your spirit I will always stand.
From my heart I chose to love you.

Joy and peace longsuffering
my faith will carry me.
On Your Word, I am secured.
Walking in Your light
Walking in Your light.

Gentleness and goodness.
My faith will carry me.
Meekness and temperance.
Walking in Your light.
Walking in Your light.

Walking in Your light, I will bear fruit.
Walking Your light, I will bear fruit.

Reflection

There is something quite remarkable, and therapeutic to see, when trees and "plant like seeds" blossom, and bloom in the vibrancy of spring. Other than producing fruits, trees as you will see them all around, are vital to the conservation of the planet and all manner of life. For the environment, they provide a visual appeal for which many can enjoy, for every season. Depending on the climate, soil, and the root, the fruits they produce, can turn out to be just right or not so ripe. On the day of reaping, succulent fruits like oranges, apples, peaches, and berries are ready to be harvested. When that time comes, and you finally take a bite, the sweet juices fill your mouth beyond anything you could have expected or imagine. Other than another bite, there is nothing else you would want more. As you are satisfied and refreshed, something even more exceptional is happening on the inside. You cannot see it, but as you go about your day, living and breathing, you can feel it in your energy. You feel it morning after morning. Your skin seems brighter. Your hair texture is rich in color and touch. Your visit to the physician looks promising, and you cannot help but feel revitalized. Gradually, it dawns on you that your health has significantly improved. It takes you awhile to pinpoint what is happening, but you soon recognize your newfound energy is contributed to the fruits you have been eating. And it is all thanks to the tree from which it came.

The true quality of a tree originates from the root. If the tree is planted in good soil, it will flourish. If it is in the wrong climate and environment, it will not survive.[1]

A healthy body and a healthy ministry are just as good as the root,

Nature in all is splendor and glory can be breath taking, especially when trees flourish under the right climate. Within the context of the bible, there are key symbolic lessons which teach about the spiritual and physical aspects of trees in comparison to the human/Christian life. Central to the theme of existence, it was a tree by which Adam and Eve had a choice to either live or die. With respects to fruits, the term is made in reference to the characteristics of those who *walk in the spirit, and not in the flesh* (Romans 8:4).

In Galatians, Paul highlights the evidence (fruit) of one who lives by the Spirit: *"But the fruit of the Spirit is love, joy, peace, longsuffering, gentleness, goodness, faith, Meekness, temperance: against such there is no law"* (Galatians 5:22-23).

With relation to the quality of such a fruit, Psalm 1 describes that there are those who are blessed when they *"reject the advice of the wicked"* but they take delight in God's Law (His word). *"They are like trees planted by streams —they bear their fruit in season, their leaves never wither, everything they do succeeds"* (Tehillim (Psa) 1:1-3 ᶜᴶᴮ).

Like a tree planted in good soil, when you live by the rivers of water (in Gods word), you grow, and when the time is right you produce the organic qualities of the spirit. With Jesus as your light like the sun, you will blossom and bloom in your season, and those who harvest from your branches, will also be blessed. They will be blessed when you love. They will be blessed when you love with joy, peace, longsuffering, goodness, faith, meekness, and temperance. You are also blessed because your walk in Christ is gradually perfected.

Your song is as strong as your Root; therefore, strengthen your root as you live.

Nourished by the anointed joy,
always blooming in the core of peculiar times,
[you] maintain it well so that [you] may sing to the glory of the Father.

Today you can sing the Lord's song "Walking in your light, I will bear fruit"

Scripture Reference
Galatians 5:22-23 ♦ Ephesians 5:9 ♦ Psalms 1:3

Your Day's Reflection

_____

_____

_____

_____

_____

_____

_____

_____

_____

I Lay my Burdens Down

Cast thy burden upon the Lord, and he shall sustain thee:
he shall never suffer the righteous to be moved.
♦ **Psalm 55:22**

Heaviness in the heart of man maketh it stoop
but a good word maketh it glad.
♦ **Proverbs 12:25**

THE VERSE

Lord, here I am,
here I stand.
Boldly I come to Your throne,
to lay down my burdens for these cast down bones.

For many days, thinking, thinking.
I believe I can manage the balance of the weight.
It seems light enough in the hands of my gait.

I believe if I am strong enough,
If I am smart enough,
If I am wise enough,
I may come out victorious.

Along the way, my garment is torn and tried.

My back gets pressed against a merciless, with chattering teeth.
My tears fall and accuse the ground as they descend.

All these things I feel and see are an extension of a very troubled world.

By faith and grace, unto Thee Oh Lord, do
I lift my cares and my burdens.
Lay them down I do, at Your feet.

Whilst the rains spare none, one droplet,
multiplies and drenches the valley.

The chuckles of rumors whisper my name.
Calling me to give up and never live to see another day.

Through it all, I seek Your voice.
Through it all, I seek Your face.

Amid fogs blooming white
distorting my eyesight.
What I see and hear is only bursting with the what-ifs.

Hidden in caves filled with dark and gaping holes.
It is Your peace which brings the comfort
to nourish the starvation of my soul.
"Out of this," you say. *"You'll come to the other side."*

In my prayers, it makes a chorus.
It tells me the coming verdict like a feather tickling my ear.
I can be blessed to know these problems won't last here.

Through the land, upon which my body has traversed.
Some burdens are good for me, because one
day I can smile at them again.

On the altar my tears are shed for you my Lord.

In my Lord, the answer is due.

Making me stronger I continue to lift the weights.
For I know You'll never give me more than I can bare.

Confessing out my heart, I empty the contents.
I lay down the guilt that have easily beset.
I release the regret for what I couldn't do.
I brace confidence by the handles and ride out the storm.

For the food, I search.
For the shelter over my head
anxious, anxious I shall not be.
I will wait on you Lord for the blessings you'll bestow.

Here I stand.
Boldly I come to Your throne,
to lay my burdens for these downtrodden bones.

Unto thee Oh Lord, do I lift my burdens
and lay them down I do at Your feet.

YOUR SONG

God, Here I am before You
Right here on my knees
With a heart still yearning for Your grace and mercy
Lord, you know all my thoughts, and you know my needs
So, I lay my concerns here at Your feet
I will cast all my cares on You my because You care for me
There is nothing too big or nothing too small for you to handle
When my heart is overwhelmed, you are my solid rock
In the time of trouble, you are my present help
I give it all to You

Reflection

I WILL SING TO LAY MY BURDENS DOWN
I lift my burdens and lay them down at Your feet

Arrayed with countless uncertainties, and temptations, there are days when problems are always floating around. Distresses of all kinds come from any and every direction. Some you are prepared to brace, while others take residence in your being and reach a point where you go quiet, numb, and even depressed. It is then that you cry out for help and are just not sure how to get it. It crosses your mind to pray, but what comes out your mouth is, *"why me?"* or *"what is left for me to do?"* Burdens, as you know them to be, do come in different shapes and sizes. Synonymous with loads and weights, some are more beneficial, while others are not so good. It could also be a combination of the two. But then there comes a time when specific pressures and or concerns can become too much.

It is often said for growth and development, some problems – whatever they may be – only come to make you stronger. While it could be that easy to acknowledge and accept such truths, burdens, if not taken care of, can change you.

Have you been carrying a weight? A load. A particular burden for so long that it has left you so numb, your heart beats with a stooped rhythm of something you cannot describe? Is what your carrying bursting to be released. Are you ready to let it go?

For three women, and one man, these afflictions, and burdens came in the form of grief, bullying, and long-lasting health infirmities. Naomi, the mother-in-law to Ruth and Orpah, had been sourly grieved about the death of her two sons (Mahlon & Chilion) and her husband, Elimelech. She told her fellow brethren, *"Do not call me Naomi; call me Mara, for the Almighty has dealt very bitterly with me. I went away full, and the Lord has brought me back empty"* (Ruth 1:20a ESV).

I Want to Sing Your Song

For Hannah, her burden was two-fold. She had to deal with the likes of Peninnah (her husband's second wife) and the consistent reminder of her childlessness. Considerably a bully, Peninnah [provoked] Hannah "grievously" *for years*. This burden led Hannah to weep and pray to the point that Eli the priest thought she was drunk (1 Samuel 1).

The woman with the issue of blood spent all she had on medical expenses, but none of them could give her the healing she needed (Luke 8:43).

Then there was the man who had an "*an infirmity of thirty-eight years.*" Due to his limited mobility, each time the angel would come and trouble the water, he would miss his chance for healing (John 5:1-7).

For each of these conditions, they demonstrated how burdens of affliction, heartache, and distresses prove to be very burdensome. You could be a Naomi grieved by a great loss. You could be Hannah with a Peninnah in your life who will not let you forget about your condition. You could be the woman with the issue of blood, where medical solutions prove to be futile. You could be the man by the poolside with a burden of thirty-eight years where no one sees and will help you. But as trouble will be, there is a thread of hope for each of these situations. Naomi gained a new family. Hannah gained a son who became a judge. Both the woman and the man afflicted with health issues were made whole.

While it would seem, you are alone carrying this burden, you can rest assure, Jesus, your great burden bearer, is always concerned about what causes you distress." *He is touched with the feelings of our infirmities*" (Hebrews 4:15). For your grief, distress, frustrations, afflictions, and pain, you can:

lay your burdens down and lay them down at Jesus feet.

TODAY, YOU CAN SING THE LORD'S SONG, "... I
LAY MY CONCERNS HERE AT YOUR FEET"

Scripture Reference
**Psalm 55:22 ♦ Proverbs 12:25 ♦ Ruth 1:20 ♦ 1 Samuel
1 ♦ Luke 8:43 ♦ John 5:1-7 ♦ Hebrews 4:15**

Your Day's Reflection

_____

_____

_____

_____

_____

_____

_____

_____

_____

Faith is the Substance

Now faith is the substance of things hoped for, the evidence of things not seen
♦ **Hebrews 11:1**

For as the body without the spirit is dead, so faith without works is dead also
♦ **James 2:26**

THE VERSE

From the substance of the account.
From the testimony of the witness.
By the call of One Voice,
these four Fathers made their choice.

With one step, they set their tent to go forth,
They set their choice to go either east, west, south, or north

By wonders of wonders,
before the foundations,
faith gave the song for saints
who suffered hard and long.

You gave Adam the domain
and You gave Eve the promised child.

Surrounded by those of incomplete soundness,

Alitta P.S Cadmus & Melissea M Walters

they allowed their ears to hear what You would tell them.

For many born of sorrows,
and of woes, the days come and go.

A choice to live on, it is the substance of Faith's goal.

Somethings might remain a mystery.
The struggle to push past the restraint of limits,
may ruffle the wings.
Soaring to higher heights,
and deeper depths,
looking down it might not make sense.

In this matter, the substance is the hope to know:
Step by step,
Day by day,
For cares of tomorrow,
I can still lift my faith.

You gave Abram the vision of the nations of sand and stars.
By logic, he could not see that far.
Nevertheless, by one footprint after another,
he paved the way to be the nation's Father.

You gave Noah the future of the abundance of rain.
Many mocked and sneered.
But for his household, he maintained his faith.

Faith of brothers,
Faith of sisters.
Holding hands, they kept the risk.
They made their decision.
Into the ark of deliverance, they came.

Floods after suns and moons after stars

You gave the leaf a promise,
bowing in colors of tomorrow's tune.

Gaining my good report,
I close my eyes, take this risk, and step on the water
as You call

Step by Step,
Day by day,
for cares of tomorrow,
I can still lift my faith.

YOUR SONG

Step by step and day by day
I am living by faith
I am living by faith
Though I cannot see it
I still believe
I am living by faith,
I am living by faith

Lord, you know my future and every way I take.
So, I will move forward, keeping my eyes on you
I may not have all the answers, or know what tomorrow may bring
But I will depend, completely on you

Reflection

I am living by faith, though I cannot see it, I still believe

Standing on the edge of the blissful sea, you can see the horizon underlining the mountains. The wind tosses the waves, as their soft caps reach your feet. The thought is in your heart to take this risk and step out. The call has been laid on your heart to start the business, write the book, write the song, go back to school. Even though you may be confronted with excuses for why you should not do this, there is a touch of faith on your heart. Taking the bull by the horn, you venture out into the unknown, stepping into new territory. Well on your way, you are in your element doing what it is you do. Favorable business deals knock at your door, and it seems there is nowhere else to go but up. Then halfway through, a voice comes and pings your logic to ask the question

"What has possessed me to do this?"

The critic in your plan maps out all the reasons as to why you should quit while you are ahead. The task no longer seems like a dream to catch. The struggle has become real; the discouragement and minor disappointment race your heart. Uninvited fear depicts in your mind the pending doom of embarrassment shame, humiliation, and loss. Unable to see beyond the doubt, you begin to feel foolish. You wonder to yourself; *do you have what it takes to make it!* Yet, amid all these uncertainties, faith comes in like a whispered song saying, *"Yes, you can!"*

To live a fulfilled life, to make it through the hard times. To take those big leaps. All you really need is a *little bit of faith*.

The heroes of faith actively pleased the Lord by their obedience and trust in His word.

Adam was instructed to "name the animals" (Genesis 2).

Abram heard, "Get thee out of thy country" (Genesis 12).

Noah heard, " Make yourself an ark," (B'resheet (Gen) 6:14 ^CJB).

Peter heard, "Come" (Matthew 14:29).

From such testimonies, faith was the vehicle to propel these men and women of old to do things that did not make sense. Whether they complained or not, Abram still packed his belongings, including his family, and left Haran without any evidence of whether his journey would be a success. All he had was the word of a great future, and the vision of a city whose builder and maker were God.

Noah built the Ark in spite of how it would've looked to his family and the community (Genesis 5-6).

Peter upon which the church was built, braced against the laws of physics and reality. Whatever compelled him, he asked, "*Lord if it is you bid me come.*" For a small but most prolific act, Peter – whom some would say was out of his mind - stepped out of the boat. His feet touched the impeccable surface of deep waters, and just like that, he walked toward Jesus. It was for a short while, and Jesus pulled him up from the uncompromising depths. Disappointing as it were, Jesus did not disregard the "*little faith*" his disciple had. It just meant this moment was to be a lesson for Peter about not losing faith (Matthew 14:27-31).

Although some had yet to obtain the promise, they still died with the conviction of better things to come.

Faith is a process, and it does come with experience. With each new challenge and opportunity you will be tested, and it will not always be easy. You will feel emotions that rub against your resilience to hold on and push through. There will come moments when you will ask yourself the question, "Am I out of my mind?" While you would have doubts, faith still generates the belief that what you hope for has already taken place. Key in your walk with God, if you do not have the confidence or believe in His abilities, it becomes that much more difficult to please Him. You will question everything (like time, when, how). You will put yourself in the position to distrust His word when He says, "Yes...Wait!" or "Go!"

When your resolve might break, and you feel to let go, you can look to the testimonies of faith from Abram, Peter, Noah, and all the men and women of old.

Whatever it is the Lord has promised, Praise
Him for it now, for it is already done.

Step by Step
Day by day
For cares of tomorrow
[you] can still lift [your] faith

TODAY YOU CAN SING THE LORD'S SONG "I AM LIVING BY FAITH
THOUGH I CANNOT SEE IT
I STILL BELIEVE"

Scripture Reference
Hebrews 11 ♦ James 2:26 ♦ Matthew 14: 27-31

Your Day's Reflection

_____

_____

_____

_____

_____

_____

_____

_____

_____

I Put My Trust in You

*Trust in the Lord with all thine heart; and lean
not unto thine own understanding.*
♦ **Proverbs 3:5**

Blessed is the man that trusteth in the Lord, and whose hope the Lord is.
♦ **Jeremiah 17:7**

What time I am afraid, I will trust in thee ♦ **Psalm 56:3**

THE VERSE

In this moment, in the room, in the silence,
my soundness twists and turns to dislodge out of place.

Creeping noise grab my ankle.
Pulling, pulling, they try to dismantle.

But my mind is anchored on the trust.
By the stroke of midnight stars, You will not fail.

Somehow,
You will,
You will deliver me.

As I tremble through the narrow crevices of ventured crossroads.

My feet go along the fine line.
On each side, I am enclosed.

The voices and eyes await
anticipating what you will do.
My trust engages me to choose or refuse.

From these ponderings of practicality, it is always asked,
will You come through?
Will You heal me when mortality is called?
Will You deliver me when my back is pressed against a wall?
As I gasp in a wholesome breath, I remind myself of the time past.

So simple, so easy.
My hands do itch to run from Your tight control.
I can steer the condition into what I know.
Like the Mary of Martha and of Lazarus,
I waver from the past and the present.

Inwardly I reason that without these fires,
I would be well.
In place of comfort,
I would be safe from tried and fails.
In my coherence, and without Your presence, I would've figured it out.

I may or cannot understand what this is before me.
I may try to figure out the shadows brighten by the light.
Even in this I try to remind myself, "It will be alright."
I try to remind myself You will answer when Your Name is called.

Unlike man, You tell no lies.
For in Your nature,
You do not waste words floating about like flies.

Wholesome You are by merit and favour.
You demonstrate that no matter what we do,

Your words will never falter like-kind gestures.

For that which I desire to do,
I must always remember to acknowledge you.
There will be times when I am lost and cannot find my way.
And I'll struggle for a while, and until I
recognize, I can't do this any other way.
I know I can trust in Your voice among the numbers of crowds.
For others like me shout the promise of being found.

Lonesome darksome are these times.
I pray for faith to be the vehicle to drive into the believe.
I let go of my inhibitions and know my life is in Your hands.

From all, You have said,
From all, You have done,
Despite how I feel,
Despite what You may not have done,
gracious of wondrous ways,
glorious by the clouds of stars,
I decide.
I choose to put my trust in You.

YOUR SONG

I put my trust in You
I put my trust in You
There is nothing impossible for You God
I put my trust in You
My life is in Your hands
On Your Word I will stand
There is nothing impossible for you God,
I put my trust in You

Reflection

Alongside faith, trust is the maintained belief (the confidence) in a person's ability, integrity, and strength in what they say they will do and what they will not do. Like love, it is the life-giving element for which a relationship will grow. There is an opacity of transparency that involves honesty and trustworthiness. Like a clear-crystal glass, once broken, it can be nearly impossible to recover. Subjective to an individual's confidence, trust can be that easy, while for others it is a process. It could be derived by natural experiences or substantiated by word of bond. When someone says, "You can trust me." Basically, they are asking you to take them at their word. They are asking you to give them a chance, as you make yourself vulnerable to their prerogative. When you take the time to really think about what that means, you will understand that trust is to be handled with care.

When you choose to trust, you are granting yourself the opportunity to believe even when you cannot see.

From the book of proverbs, it reads: "*Trust in the Lord with all your hearts; And lean not unto you own understanding; In all your ways acknowledge Him, and He shall direct your path*" (Proverbs 3:5-6).

In the well-known Psalm, David denotes that God is our hiding place: "*I will say of the LORD, He is my refuge and my fortress: my God; in him will I trust*" (Psalm 91:2).

From both scriptures, it is underlined that when you are faced with the unknown, or what seems impossible, it is in those times you can put your trust in God. Because He can see the things you cannot, He is more than able to direct your path.

Travelling, which is integrated into your regular and extracurricular activities, is provided by different means of transportation. These include bicycle, car, bus, plane, train, and or boat. When you leave your home and begin your journey, the knowledge and practical laws of engineering, are more than likely far from your mind. Unless, of course, you are the driver. With feelings of anticipation (depending on where you are going), you have already reached your journey's end. In fact, the most you are concerned about is when you will get there.

Similar to flying in a plane, heading towards your desired and expected destination, as a believer in Christ, your life and soul is on a course to an "*expected end*" (Jeremiah 29:11b). Sometimes, however, your trust in God can be compromised because of fear and misunderstanding. His character is equated with the disappointments of the past. His integrity and ability are even compared to other people's failures. But just as how you will hardly ever try to take control of the plane, the same trust can be applied to Jesus. With Him being the pilot, steering your life in the direction it ought to go, you can buckle in while trusting Him. He is more than able to steer you through all the thunderous clouds and boisterous winds.

It might take you some time to hold on to this truth, but you can trust and believe that God is not like man that He should lie (Jeremiah 17:7-8). "*For he shall give his angels charge over thee, to keep thee in all thy ways. They shall bear thee up in their hands, lest thou dash thy foot against a stone*" (Psalms 91:11-12). He will never change who He is or give false impressions just to deceive you. Time might persuade otherwise, but it is of an assurance, His word "*It shall not return unto me void, but it shall accomplish that which I please...*" (Isaiah 55:11a)

Wholesome [He is] by merit and favour.
[He] demonstrates that no matter what we do,
[His] words will never falter like-kind gestures…

TODAY YOU CAN SING THE LORD'S SONG OF HIS SINCERITY:
"THERE IS NOTHING IMPOSSIBLE FOR YOU GOD
I PUT MY TRUST IN YOU"

Scripture Reference
Psalms 56:3 ♦ Isaiah 55:11 ♦ Proverbs 3:5-6 ♦
Jeremiah 17:7-8; 29:11 ♦ Psalms 91:11-12

I Want to Sing Your Song

Your Day's Reflection

_____

_____

_____

_____

_____

_____

_____

_____

_____

Oh, Grace, Grace, Grace

*But he said to me, "My grace is sufficient for you, for my power is
made perfect in weakness." Therefore, I will boast all the more gladly
about my weaknesses, so that Christ's power may rest on me.*
♦ ***2 Corinthians 12:9***

*For by grace are ye saved through faith; and that
not of yourselves: it is the gift of God:*
♦ **Ephesians 2:8**

THE VERSE

From this time of need,
to the crown of my head.
To the soles of these burdened down feet.
The pursuance of my weakness,
pants for the succulent rivers of compassions.

Flowing from the stream, through the portals,
it is grace which gives me the rock to stand on.

Oh grace, grace, grace.
The helping hand when troubles come knocking.

Oh grace, grace, grace.
The comforting arms from a mother's touch.

A sacred stone You are displayed for all eyes to see,
In the smile of a child, in the voice of an angel
You are the *sweet melody.*

On the pages of great decades,
are the telling's of the amazing perseverance of the Holy heart.
Venturing into the prison,
You unshackled the precious mortals confounded
by the clouds of lawless pestilence.

Swift with the trembling of the earth, by the sword
You pierce the underbelly of the contemptuous beast.

By the wayside of binary seasons,
the tears fall as the sorrows fade and come.
For the bleak, and uncertain souls
You have become the stream
for which the love constantly flows.

Oh grace, grace, grace.
You rewrote the sentence of condemnation,
You served yourself to the death
to collect the accursed wages.

Though tossed and turned by the ways of despair,
You humble my pride so that I can grab a hold of the beauty
at prayer-filled bedsides.

Complacent I was from discoveries to do it all wrong.
But *Oh Grace, Grace, Grace*
You are the staff to lean upon.
By you I 'am blessed.

When the *"loud noise spreads across
and crosses back again"*,
the silence of serenity

gives the shelter to hide in peace.

The Sunlight through the cracks.
The New Growth out of crevices,
you mend these wounds
so, I can be the bridge
to show the way to ultimate forgiveness.

Oh, Grace, Grace, Grace.

Carrying me to purpose and giving me the strength to do.
I have the faith to stay in the honour of my Fathers shoes.

This bestowal,
This undeserved,
Unearned,
Unrequested,
Is grace, grace, grace
Oh, Grace, Grace, Grace

YOUR SONG

Thank You, Lord, for grace, Your grace.
Lord, Your grace has opened the way, the way.
The key to everlasting hope.
Lord, Your grace.
I would have never made it without Your grace.
hank you, Lord, for grace, Your grace
Lord, Your grace has opened the way, the way
The key to everlasting hope
Lord, Your grace
I would have never made it without Your grace
I Thank You Lord, for Your Grace.

Reflection

*Grace. Grace. Grace. What could be said other than it is
truly a gift? What could anyone ever do to deserve it?*

Have you ever had a rough day that wiped you of your strength and peace of mind? It made you feel like all the life was drained out of you. Then like a cold refreshing drink of pure, satisfying waters, someone smiles at you. They stare into your eyes and say,

"Come, I will help you get through this. Come, I will be with you every step of the way. Come, I'll help you carry that burden. Let me sing this song for your heart."

Such words are quite reassuring especially when the *times* look as if it will get you down. But like an anchor, *"grace, grace, grace"* secures the mind and heart. In songs, in words of comfort, by a hug, it nurtures your spirit to know, *"You will make it out of this. You will get through the midnight hours of shadows and dimmed lights."*

One of those things needed but not earned; grace does not need permission to come. Like a balm, it helps you to deal with thorns that burn your flesh. Most of all, grace is that new-found joy in the morning. A voice speaking with virtue, it pronounces, *"Arise, you can live again."*

Consigned with faith, trust, and a prayer-filled life, grace, has consistently been that staff that holds up the weakest.

Paul, who committed himself to expound on the gospel of Christ, found himself having to deal with a situation that required a lot of *grace*.

Carrying his burden to the Lord, he expressed how this troubled him greatly:

"Therefore, to keep me from becoming overly proud, I was given a thorn in my flesh, a messenger from the Adversary to pound away at me, so that I

wouldn't grow conceited. Three times I begged the Lord to take this thing away from me."
(2 Corinthians (2 Co) 12:7-8 ᶜᴶᴮ).

A thorn in the flesh, is never pleasant, even if it is something to make you stronger. In Paul's case it was literally, a messenger from the Devil himself. Begging for his distress, *three times,* Paul got his answer from the Lord who said *"… My grace is sufficient for thee: for my strength is made perfect in weakness"* (2 Corinthians 12:9a).

Now one thing to consider is this, Paul sought the Lord more than once because of this thorn. This meant he was dealing with a burden that had him on his knees consistently. For him to receive *"my grace is sufficient,"* it must have been unexpected and disappointing. Anyone in Paul's shoes would, without a doubt, lament and argue, *"what do you mean? Why won't you remove this thorn from my flesh?"* Some would pray even more, saying, *"God, please remove this thing!"*

But Paul, evidently strong and of great faith, decided to accept that answer. He replied saying, *"Therefore, I am very happy to boast about my weaknesses, in order that the Messiah's power will rest upon me..."* (2 Corinthians (2 Co) 12:9a ᶜᴶᴮ).

Admittedly hard to learn, there are some situations that God will not necessarily take you out of, but He will apply His grace and mercy to get you through it. It will hurt more than you can explain, but by this you can be encouraged. *For nothing can genuinely develop without true testing.* In other cases, grace is needed for forgiveness; it is needed for another chance, especially when all doors have closed on you.

By grace many are saved. It is the gift given, not for sin to abound, but for you to arise and live again.

This bestowal,
This undeserved,
Unearned,
Unrequested,
Is grace, grace, grace.

TODAY, YOU CAN SING THE LORD'S SONG OF GRACE "LORD,
YOUR GRACE HAS OPENED THE WAY, THE WAY.
THE KEY TO EVERLASTING HOPE."

Scripture Reference
2 Corinthians 12:7-9 ♦ Ephesians 2:8

Your Day's Reflection

_____

_____

_____

_____

_____

_____

_____

_____

_____

By Prayer and Supplication

Be anxious for nothing, but in everything by prayer and supplication, with thanksgiving, let your requests be made known to God; and the peace of God, which surpasses all understanding, will guard your hearts and minds through Christ Jesus.♦ **Philippians 4:6-7**

Rejoice always, pray without ceasing, in everything give thanks; for this is the will of God in Christ Jesus for you ♦ **1 Thessalonians 5:16-18**

Let us therefore come boldly unto the throne of grace, that we may obtain mercy, and find grace to help in time of need
♦ **Hebrews 4:16**

In this manner, therefore, pray: Our Father in heaven, Hallowed be Your name. ♦ **Matthew 6:9-13**

THE VERSE

On the whispers of countless groanings,
my spirit sings for the greatest dawning.
For it knows the manifestation of dreams,
draping across the history of heavens beams.

In the hands of bruised skins,
the cries of fathers' lament for their kin.

On the countenance of howling warriors.
drunkenness seems to be the narrative.
For their cries, expose the spill of their kind's blood.

With much to say, it is sounded high on praises.
In the mouth of determined weeping mothers,
a prayer of deliverance gives a shout.

Silk tears emerge from bowels of soundless words.
Such is the deepest of concerns:
let there to be a revealing of the deceit adorned in silk-like fabrics.

The sounds say enough, because
only You understand the language of tears,
which the soul and spirit whimper.

On the knees, bended is prostrate.
Nothing else to give, in the throat,
the weight is much of the bundled grief.

In the devotions of lamentations,
it is for Your tender love the supplication beseechs.

Deliverer of the thousands.
Pillar for the multitude
Surround this place.
This is the prayer.
This is the cry.
For my home needs deliverance.

From the cry of the root, anchored is the contrition.
There is no other way but to lean on you.

A friend for the helpless.
A brother for the lowliest.
In You, is sought the right way.

So that the feet can walk the way of holiness

Far and wide it is hard to know.

In my weakness, it's not my will that will sustain,
but it's by Your divine interventions for which I must pray.

I pray, intercede.
I bewail

Oh, let these prayers reach heavens stairs.
Climb to the throne for my father hears.
Let him hear me and us as we say

No matter the time
No matter the day

I beseech for deliverance
I hold on for my endurance
I cry for my healing
I prostate my salvation
I pray Your Lord's Song of deliverance.
So, at this moment,
I stop and devote these supplications unto you

YOUR SONG

I pray for my deliverance
I pray for my endurance
I pray for my healing
I pray for my salvation

I lay my burdens down
I lay my burdens down
At your feet

We pray and You deliver
We pray and You restore
It's not according to man to direct his own life
So, I have to pray
It's not according to man to direct his life
So, I have to pray

Hmmm so I have to pray (oh yes, so pray)
So, I have to pray

Reflection

I WILL SING THE PRAYERS IN MERCY HALLS
I pray the Lord's song of deliverance

At the core of who you are, there is a treasurable gift to communicate. Socially structured, you have the capability to exchange information through the function of the body. These areas include verbal, non-verbal, written and listening. In social relationships, these key areas of communication serve as the channels for external and internal expression. When you are relating to other people, what you say and or hear, help you to build interpersonal and impersonal relationships. For some of the things you have to say, there are times when you will need to make a request. You will need to make an appeal. But for the most part, social interactions are the channel for opened and closed communication. It is not only about what is said, but rather what is heard. In the event when you need to make the right response, it is important that you understand the other side so that when you respond, you know what you are saying. If it requires an action, you know what you are doing.

Prayer is a part of every believer's way of communicating with God.

Just as how we interact with one another, our Heavenly Father wants the same thing with His children. He wants to have meaningful and intentional conversations with us.

This is ordinarily done in the form of worship. There is a reverence which connects you to the Holy Spirit. On such grounds, you can *"seek"* the Lord's face and give your supplications. From His teachings, Jesus gives the divine structure of how to pray.

Our Father in heaven, Hallowed be Your name.
Your kingdom come. Your will be done
On earth as it is in heaven. Give us this day our daily bread.
And forgive us our debts, As we forgive our debtors.
And do not lead us into temptation, But deliver us from the evil one.

For Yours is the kingdom and the power and the glory forever. Amen
(Matthew 6:9-13).

Many quote this prayer as a substitute to pray; however, it is not meant to take the place of proper communication with the Heavenly Father. Nonetheless it is still a powerful template of what to say. While you can put in your request, and appeal for the things that you need help with - like with a friend - prayer basically is the platform for divine fellowship. During such times, you are committing yourself to dwell (spend time) in the presence of the Lord. He who sees and knows all things, does listen, and responds when you pray. Even though the Lord already knows what you are going to say, He will graciously give you the space to say, whatever it is you need (or want) to tell Him.

At the same time, you also must be ready to hear what He will say in return. Usually, this can be hard. It is not all the time when someone responds to your concerns, appeals, and or desires, you get the response you want.

Just as important as the other aspects for spiritual health, and livelihood, prayer serves as a channel for the things you need. This could be grace, a little bit of strength, some form of direction, and a touch of faith.

Observed and explain in the Holman Study bible, there are "three words" that define the different aspects of prayer: [1] *Prayer* is a worshipful attitude while you give your [2] *supplication* for a specific request. [3] *Thanksgiving shapes* your attitude as you pray. [1]

While prayer is your way to talk to God, it also serves as a ground for which you can gain strength, and peace for your journey toward the heavenly promise. With the permission to come boldly unto *the throne of grace," In* your time of need, *"you obtain mercy, and find grace"* (Hebrews 4:16). By grace your inner being is renewed merely by the thought of knowing God hears you. As it is encouraged do not stop talking to Jesus; *pray without ceasing* (1 Thessa 5:17) for He can hear you.

For your home and family:
… *pray for deliverance*
…*pray for endurance*
…*pray for healing*
… *pray for salvation*

TODAY YOU CAN SING THE LORD'S SONG OF
PRAYER. "I PRAY FOR MY DELIVERANCE"

Scripture Reference
**Psalms 126:5 ♦ Philippians 4:6-7 ♦ 1 Thessalonians
5:16-18 ♦ Hebrews 4:16 ♦ Matthew 6:9-13**

_____

_____

_____

_____

_____

_____

_____

_____

_____

Part 1: I 'am Walking in a Brand-New Life

Therefore, if any man be in Christ, he is a new creature: old things are passed away; behold, all things are become new ♦ **2 Corinthians 5:17**

THE VERSE

Once upon a time,
the wayside of life was the earned reputation.
The beginnings of one breath
became the population of a generation
and a nation of races
made after the kind of ill-repute.

The vision was blocked in the wondering and lost way,
nor could the eyes see the light.

Despite the fall, respite came in the form of Christ.
His broken body became the price for the blood-bought cause.

Now the honour is given to the souls of men to push back and fight.
For in Christ, we are the new creature, set upon a hill to shine bright.

I' am walking in a brand-new life
I'm a new creation.

Once upon a time, hope did stand afar off, and
I wept for what was to come and be.
Now, as History is retold through complete chapters and verses.
The hymn becomes the ground upon which I stand.

Once upon a time, I had been a pot,
I was a vessel marred by picks up and drops.

My innocence broke; it had smashed to the ground.
Pieces scattered separated and divided, seemingly
not to be put back together again.

Intended for the soul, there is an anchor for me to join ranks.
With wisdom, knowledge, and understanding,
the spirit, which is the element of heaven,
is the kind of Christ.
In Him, the new life begins.

Determine to hold out, I adhere to the will of God.
At His table, I 'am fed well by the daily bread.
Along my way, on the pilgrim journey,
I cannot let the blindness block that which is set before me.

Foreign places shall welcome.
Foreign places might enfold me.

With comfort it is only but for the temporary.

I might be robbed disgracefully,
and my hands become involved,
behind bars of a wall suffocating my liberty.

Even so, I 'am washed in His blood.
I have been revived.
I must not forget who I am,
nor the cleansing flood that redefines.

According to His mercy, I am saved

I am no longer the ashes buried in sin.

I am conformed by a power
I have become the condensation of new birth.

Coming from the womb of uncertainty,
the Lord still possesses my reins.
He holds my heart for His to claim.

From His might, He opens the prison of condemnation.
With a loud bang the door creaks
as the old things of the past become new.

The ricochet of finality echoes across the halls,
never to be heard of again.

Possessed in the palm of the Master's hands,
I am walking in a brand-new life, I am a new creation.

YOUR SONG

I 'am walking in a brand-new life
I'm a new creation
I 'am walking in a brand-new life
I'm a new creation

I've been washed in the blood
of Jesus Christ
The old way is gone I've been revived

I 'am walking in a brand-new life
I'm a new creation

Reflection

I WILL SING FOR BEHOLD ALL THINGS BECOME NEW
I am the new creation formed in Christ.

Out with the old in with the new, is a phrase commonly expressed within the context of when something is being thrown out. Springtime, which is a season many look forward to, customarily generates the need for individuals to spring clean. Items are either refurbished, thrown out and or replaced. This process stems from the need to change the environment in which you live, and function. There is an internal motivation to move on from the former things that have lost their quality. Similar to the renovation of a building or home, individuals will seek for methods to change their physical appearance. It is a common belief that once a person changes who they are on the outside, it is expected he or she will feel good about who they are on the inside. Then there is of course a life transformation, which takes on the totality of a person. This could include a change of environment. Change of wardrobe. Change of behaviour. Change of the people who are in your life. Change of how you think, process, and interpret the world around you.

For a caterpillar to fly, it must shed its old skin.
For a tree to bare new fruit it must shed the old leaves

When a person gives their life to Jesus - *transitions from living the old life of sin to the new* - a beauty is manifested *through the fruits of the spirit* (Galatians 5:22-25).

This fruit is developed in the nature of individuals and is demonstrated in how we talk and walk. In Christ, we have the principle to know and understand, that it is not so much what is on the outside that needs to change, but it is that which is on the inside. Written for the church it is stated in scripture, *"Therefore, if any man be in Christ, he is a new creature: old things are passed away; behold, all things are become new"* (2 Corinthians 5:17).

To experience a make-over and be transformed to the structure and nature of Christ, there is a process free to all men. It involves believing that Jesus is Lord; repenting; being reborn (cleansed) through water baptism and being filled with the Holy Spirit.

Like a caterpillar, that crawls on the ground, surrounded by dirt and pending dangers, there comes a time when metamorphosis will occur, and the old skin sheds off. Known as metamorphosis, it is explained as a "transformation; the marked change in some animals at a stage in their growth." [1]

In winter, plant-like seeds of trees, bushes, and flowers shed off old leaves that have dried up. This process helps the tree conserve water and energy. Astoundingly, while the tree is bare and appears lifeless, the leaves that have fallen off, helps the tree "to survive harsh weather conditions," [2]

Even though you will make efforts to reinvent yourself, and attempt to change, you can be reassured that your transformation in Christ is not dependent on works. (Titus 3:5). But it does involve the "renewal of the mind" (Romans 12:2). It involves the process of shedding off, and eliminating the old way of thinking. This can be done by you engaging with the word of God. Or having positive conversations with the people who will help you develop into a better person.

Unlike a caterpillar or a tree, transformation is dependent on you making the choice to do so. As Christ died for you, you are no longer left to be a creature after the old nature.

There will be times when you will change and not even know it, but as you are aware of yourself and your environment, it is your ultimate decision to accept the process of change or remain just as you are. And, once you change, and walk in the newness of life, you do become a new creature, walking in a brand-new life.

There was a song you use to sing, and it served your purpose. But now, there is a new song and it is the call to be the new creature.

Now the honour is given to the souls of men to push back and fight. For in Christ, [you] are the new creature, set upon a hill to shine bright.

TODAY YOU CAN SING THE LORD'S SONG: "I'AM WALKING
IN A BRAND NEW I 'AM A NEW CREATION"

Scripture Reference
2 Corinthians 5:17 ♦ Romans 8:9 ♦ Titus 3:5

Your Day's Reflection

_____

_____

_____

_____

_____

_____

_____

_____

_____

Part 2: I Don't Have to Look Back

Brethren, I do not count myself to have [d]apprehended; but one thing I do, forgetting those things which are behind and reaching forward to those things which are ahead. I press toward the goal for the prize of the upward call of God in Christ Jesus. ♦ **Philippians 3:13-14**

"Do not remember the former things, Nor consider the things of old. Behold, I will do a new thing, Now it shall spring forth; Shall you not know it? I will even make a road in the wilderness and rivers in the desert. ♦ **Isaiah 43:18-19**

So, it came to pass, when they had brought them outside, that [b]he said, "Escape for your life! Do not look behind you nor stay anywhere in the plain. Escape to the mountains, lest you be [c]destroyed."
♦ **Genesis 19:17**

THE VERSE

Better Days are ahead.
Forward, forward I march.
Not looking back, I see the prize before me.
I lost much, but I don't have to look back anymore.
I have come too far to turn back now.

To appreciate the new,
I must learn the lesson of the life I use to live.
Between then and now,
there is a fine line that separates the choices.
It contrasts the narrow and broad-way.

In time past, I could not tell the difference between who I was then
and what cried within to go forward.

Swimming in the blissful comfort of camouflaged blessing,
I had been comfortable enough to remain.
The *old* law was to be as I was born.

By God's mercy, He has pulled me up to be saved.
He has taken my broken pieces and mended them back together again.

A new creature washed in His blood:
Old things are passed away,
and all things have become new.

I can celebrate in Jesus name for,
I am now on my way to a better Canaan.

From the string that reaches behind to who I use to be,
there are moments when a small tug urges me to look back.
Compelled by the affections of yesterday, I could do just that.

Holding on strong and with my eyes cast toward the sunrise,
I abide in Christ's word, pressing forward.

At this moment, on this day, if I am to live.
I must forget those things behind
and press forward to the glory which shall be revealed.

Mapped on the pages of hope,
there is a distinction of a bridge that connects
across to the second chance.

Comforted from the Lord's Holiness,
and bound by His love,
I can summon the courage to give thanks
for the understanding of trials, and pain.
I can understand the multitude of some seasons
speaking for themselves.

My past, which is behind me, can and will teach for itself.
The goal is not to crumble under the weight of guilt.
Nor to apprehend the object of sin's affections.

Pushing, pressing, and with the affirmation,
the dry place is no more.
There is a new abundance of purity for afflictions and infirmities.

A message of the promise given,
I can forgive to be forgiven.
I can love to be loved.
I can be the words for Jehovah's song.
Better days ahead of me...I have come too far to turn back now.

YOUR SONG

Better days are ahead of me
Pressing forward to my victory
I will not dwell on the past
A new season has come.

I don't have to look back any more
I don't have to look back any more

Better days are ahead of me
I' am pressing forward to my victory
I will not dwell on the past
A new season has come

I don't have to look back any more
I don't have to look back any more

Reflection

Sometimes when your life has changed, and you know it; you feel it, and live it, there is usually a reminder to shed light on the old. This enlightenment serves the purpose to keep you grounded, and provides the lesson to know, you can grow from your past: you can transform from your mistakes. You can grow from your experiences.

**Can you feel the change? Can you feel the shift?
Is it time to let go but you are struggling because
you are afraid of the uncertainties ahead?**

Change for a lot of people can be a wonderful thing, but sometimes transitioning into the new, can be just as discomforting. Reason being, you are challenged with the thoughts of what is ahead, like the possessions of things, and the people who use to bring you comfort.

For Lots wife, her challenge was letting go of the life she had to leave behind in Sodom and Gomorrah.

Lot, who was Abrams nephew, chose to live his life in a city where immorality and sin was quite prevalent. The land seemed flourishing and pleasing to the eye, so Lot chose it. But in God's eyes, Sodom and Gomorrah was a city that was not flourishing. It displeased Him to the point where He was going to utterly destroy it. To save Lot from the destruction, the Lord sent two angels to him.

On the morning, the angels said to Lot

"...*Arise, take your wife and your two daughters who are here, lest you be consumed in the punishment of the city.*" (Genesis 19:15b).

While he heard this, Lot delayed, and the angels had to take him, his wife and his daughters by the hand to lead them out. Before they went on their way, the angels gave this warning, "*Escape for your life! Do not look behind you nor stay anywhere in the plain. Escape to the mountains, lest you be destroyed*" (Genesis 19:17).

When they finally reached Zoar, the Lord rained down destruction on Sodom. Scary as it were, they were safe, but Lot's wife, she looked back. This action was incomprehensible because she turned into a pillar of salt. What made her condition that much more tragic, is the fact that she was delivered but died because of her choice to not look forward.

Sometimes when God comes to transition us out of destruction, we can delay our deliverance. We can hinder the blessing of transformation and or completely stop it.

When your life has been made brand new, it is imperative to recognize you are not your past. For some people, this can be difficult to accept and move on from, because usually there is always that one little reminder of what you use to be. While it is a good thing to reflect on the former things, it can equally be deadly if we do look back. And to make it as far as Lots wife did, and not be able to proceed any further can be tragic.

There is nothing wrong with remembering what has transpired years ago, because who you are is grounded in your history. From the past, you can gain lessons and wisdom that can be applied to your future life. In your understanding, and what you now know, you can appreciate what is of most value to you. Your past which used to be "new days" can be treated like memorial stars. For when you see something for what it is, you learn not to take the little or big things for granted. You learn that with each new defining moment, who you are is rooted in what you eventually become. And this is all dependent on what you choose to do: are you going to look back or go forward.

A message of the promise given,
[You] can forgive to be forgiven.
[You] can love to be loved.
[You] can be the words for Jehovah's song.
Better days ahead … [You] have come too far to turn back now.

TODAY YOU CAN SING THE LORD'S SONG: "BETTER DAYS
ARE AHEAD OF ME PRESSING FORWARD TO MY VICTORY"

Scripture Reference
Matthew 24:13 ♦ 1 Corinthians 9:24 ♦ 2 Thessalonians 3:13

_____

_____

_____

_____

_____

_____

_____

_____

Your Perfect Love

Herein is love, not that we loved God, but that he loved us, and sent His Son to be the propitiation for our sins ♦ **1 John 4:10**

For I am persuaded, that neither death, nor life, nor angels, nor principalities, nor powers, nor things present, nor things to come. Nor height, nor depth, nor any other creature, shall be able to separate us from the love of God, which is in Christ Jesus our Lord ♦ **Romans 8:38**

THE VERSE

There's no other love quite like you.
There's no other love, that rings so true.
And when I am cast down,
You come and rescue me,
and in Your love I am free.

I thought, I could love myself to the best of my integrity.
I thought, I could love others to the best of my ability.

But now, I know there is no other love that can stand,
and brace against the forces which seek and desire to take down.
There is no other love, that can restore my name;
the name of which I am called.
The name of which is my identity.

There is no other love,
that can make me feel secure and content.
Between such security, between such longsuffering,
I can bask in the freedom to weep in sincerity.

Even in the rebellious of storms,
in this love I am found carefully.
I am handled with the tenderness of touch;
reshaped back to the glory that was robbed.

A sweetness I must not lose,
I cherish it for when I am in despair.
Without condition, it picks me up
and lays me on the altar of mercy hall.

There is no other sacrifice.
There is no other burning flame.
There is no death.
There is no other arisen.
When I am chained and afflicted
You come and rescue me.

In your love
I am free.

Oh, how sweet. Oh, how revering,
is your compassion toward the helpless and blameful.
Deeming me worthy enough,
you step into the realms of cursed lands.

Like a new inhale for the imprisoned,
giving up your breath, You expelled "It is finish!",

Breathing your name,
I have become yours
now I can live on even in the rain.

A perfect love for which none can compare,
In me it flourishes;
a seed, sprouting in morning rains and dews.

There is no other love quite like you.
No other love that rings so true.
I am persuaded no height
nor depth can separate me.
For in your love, I am free.

YOUR SONG

I am yours and you are mine
You said I am the apple of your eye
Your perfect love casted out all my fears
It was your love that redeemed me and made my life complete

Nothing can separate me from the Love of God
Nothing can separate me from His love
Nothing can separate me from the Love of God
Nothing can separate me from His love.

Reflection

I WILL SING FOR I 'AM PERSUADED THERE IS NO OTHER LOVE
It was your perfect love that redeemed me

Love. What is Love? Why do we need it? How is it given? Who shows it? When is it the right time to say it? Universally, love is at the center of everything we do. It is tied to our affections and linked to the things and people we cherish. Precious as it is, many struggle to truly understand what it means to love someone other than oneself. This, in turn, makes love seem more complicated than it is. For many different people, explaining and recognizing feelings of strong affections might vary, because the actions of love might look and feel different. After all, love is not only abstractive, it is shown. Debated of what it is and or isn't, the general consensus of love rests on the hardest thing most struggle to do, and that is to love without conditions. At its center love is not self-fish, and in its totality it is life. In contemporary works of entertainment, love is often portrayed when a man and a woman experience the process of finding one another. They get married and live a happy ever after. Ideally, this would be the life to live as it does ignite exhilarating feelings of joy, contentment, and a sense of worthiness. However, the one thing that would be hard to accept and live by is the sacrificial actions of love.

**Perfectly displayed in the death of the cross,
God gave man a new way to live**

Biblically, the concept of love is quite clear: it is more giving than it receives.

In the book of John, it is written:

"For God so loved the world that He gave His only begotten Son, that whoever believes in Him should not perish but have everlasting life" (John 3:16).

The word *"so"* emphasizes the magnitude to which God loves, and while you would be counted unworthy, it does not take away how God does love you.

In the form of Jesus, He manifested his unconditional love towards mankind, so that you could live. Not based on the condition of human love, but he did it based on His condition of love. Surely, no man's love is perfect. Of a truth, sometimes loving someone other than yourself, can be hard, and not because you want it to be like that. Like everything else you strive to achieve, occasionally, it can take a while to allow yourself to feel some form of affection towards your fellowman. Written in a poetic form, we are given the nature of love, which we can strive to abide and do.

"Love suffers long and is kind...Love never fails (I Corinthians 13:4a-8).

Complex, beautiful, longsuffering and pure, God's love is endless, and there is nothing that can separate you. Nothing in the temporal or the eternal. Even though you were not searching for him, He sought after you. While human love will fail, Jesus' love supersedes all human expectations. It is real. It is strong. When you fall it is Jesus love that will pick you up, turn you around and place your feet on higher ground.

There is no other sacrifice.
There is no other burning flame.
There is no death.
There is no other arisen.
When I am chained and afflicted
You come and rescue me.

TODAY, YOU CAN SING OF THE LORD'S PERFECT LOVE
"NOTHING CAN SEPARATE ME FROM THE LOVE OF GOD"

Scripture Reference
John 15:11 ♦ Psalm 16:11 ♦ Romans 15:13
♦ Psalms 16:11 ♦ Psalms 30:5

I Want to Sing Your Song

Your Day's Reflection

I Will Drink from This Fountain

*But whosoever drinketh of the water that I shall give him shall
never thirst; but the water that I shall give him shall be in
him a well of water springing up into everlasting life.*
♦ **John 4:14**

*Blessed are those who hunger and thirst for righteousness,
For they shall be filled.* ♦ **Matthew 5:6** ^{NKJV}

*If ye then be risen with Christ, seek those things which are
above, where Christ sitteth on the right hand of God. Set your
affection on things above, not on things on the earth.*
♦ **Colossians 3:2**

THE VERSE

From the well that never runs dry,
a cup overflows.
An oil-rich with lavender,
there is a cup to drink, so I will never thirst.

In the wilderness,
the dry place suffocates the life, never to give it back.
It is a vast land where many have fallen and have risen.

Of conflictions

I Want to Sing Your Song

of derision,
the soul is taunted in turmoil.
It knows, it knows, that the earthly treasures are only temporal.

From the days of old, there is a well,
In the days of new, there is a fountain springing with new life.
Jesus sits there, waiting for me.

He knows my story from the beginning to the end.
From His cup, the water fills the empty dry places.
A vow given, in man, it will spring up into everlasting life.

There is a well that never runs dry.
There is a cup that overflows.
There is an oil-rich with lavender.
There is water to abate my thirst.

Give me this cup, oh Lord, give me this cup.
Let my tongue lavish in its refreshing grace,
so that my lungs can expand
from the suffocation of sickness and disease.

In the wilderness of the self,
exerted energy is channelled toward the legs.
It chases after visions and earthly victories:
It labours for houses, cars, lands.
Strives for riches, fame, wealth, heartfelt affections.

In all honesty, it is a cherished thought that all can satisfy.

It is an enthralling effort, to work and toil
for the sustenance of human prosperity.
In this vanity of success,
it brings comfort but lingers only for one moment.

An avoidable reality, there are two wells.

Jesus sits there, waiting for me.

From His cup, overflows the waters of everlasting life.
In me, it springs up, and in eternity it shall never run dry.

At this well where Jesus sits,
I come knowing He will not judge me.

At this well where Jesus sits,
I come knowing He hears me as I may weep.
At this well where Jesus sits,
I come knowing He will council my soul for it to be made whole.

There is a well that never runs dry.
There is a cup that overflows.
There is an oil-rich with lavender.
There is a cup to drink, so I will never thirst.

Your Song

In the wilderness of dry places there is a fountain
Springing up in me it's the waters that overflow.
Into everlasting life.

There is a well that never runs dry.
There is a cup that overflows
There is an oil rich with lavender
so, I will never thirst.

Reflection

Is there something that you are "searching" for? Is there something or someone who you believe can satisfy your needs. Are you happy living the life of prosperity? Is it enough for you to get up in the morning and do it all over again? Or do you feel that something is missing? You are grateful for the people you have in your life, but there is an emptiness. There is a loneliness. You are content for the things you have, but something is missing.

Being thirsty is a sign of dehydration. Are you thirsty?
Do you have a void that needs to be filled?

When Adam ate the forbidden fruit, a hunger and thirst generated in the bowls of mankind's soul. The affections meant for the Creator shifted to something else; we could no longer be satisfied. From this root, springing up in man, was the yearning and desires for things that could make them feel good about life. But when Jesus met the woman at the well, He confronted and addressed her thirst and hunger. Her love and affections were in the wrong place. Speaking in a language for her to understand, Jesus enlightened her with these words. *"But whosoever drinketh of the water that I shall give him shall never thirst; but the water that I shall give him shall be in him a well of water springing up into everlasting life"* (John 4:14b).

With the hint of eternity, Jesus opened the woman's eyes to recognize that the five men for which she gave her affections to were not her husband. In other words, they were earthly possessions that could not help her. And for Jesus to sit at the well, it signified the difference between living the *old life versus the new.* Jacobs well was old, but Jesus was the new well. The new fountain from which the waters would quench the thirst in man for eternity.

For the woman receiving the revelation about the man asking her for a drink, she left her water pot (symbolizing her old life) and became a professor of truth

"*Come see a man*" (John 4:29a).

A new creature, she sang the Lords song of true revelation – and a newfound relationship.

When you shift your affections from the earthly things to righteousness (walking in the spirit), you are blessed. Because then you open up yourself to be filled. Your thirst is quenched from within, and from such waters, you flourish in and out of your season. The songs you sing have a different taste. A different quality for which Jesus can appreciate.

At this well where Jesus sits, I come knowing He will not judge me.
At this well where Jesus sits, I come knowing He hears me as I may weep.
At this well where Jesus sits, I come knowing He will
council my soul for it to be made whole.

TODAY YOU CAN SING THE LORD'S SONG "THERE IS A WELL THAT NEVER RUNS DRY. THERE IS A CUP THAT OVERFLOWS"

Scripture Reference
John 4:14; 29 ♦ Revelations 7:16-17 ♦
Matthew 5:6 ♦ Colossians 3:2

Your Day's Reflection

_____

_____

_____

_____

_____

_____

_____

_____

_____

I Can Smile Again, for I 'am Blessed

*Blessed shalt thou be when thou comest in, and
blessed shalt thou be when thou goest out.*
♦ **Deuteronomy 28:6**

*They shall neither hunger anymore nor thirst anymore; the sun shall not
strike them, nor any heat; for the Lamb who is in the midst of the throne
will shepherd them and lead them to living fountains of waters. And God
will wipe away every tear from their eyes* ♦ **Revelations 7:16-17** NKJV

*Blessed are those who hunger and thirst for righteousness,
For they shall be filled.* ♦ **Matthew 5:6** NKJV

THE VERSE

Yes, the tears have soaked my pillow
holding me down as I felt inconsolable.
But with the past behind me,
and
with Jesus' refreshing love,
I can smile again, for I am blessed.

Yes, I stared through the window of possibilities,
as the moon shone bright, shading the darkness of the empty spaces.

The glow painted my walls.
Contrasting against what I could see.

I turn to the left
I turn to the right

I saw my own shadows staring back at me
But with the past behind me,
and with Jesus light, I can smile again, for I am blessed.

I prayed for forgivness.
I prayed for the distant sun to give me mercy.

Because I took my youth filled days for granted,
my house crumbled to shambles
And I didn't know how to rebuild.

But the Master articulate of beautiful creations,
reformed and transformed my dignity into integrity.
With the past behind me
and Precious Jesus holding my hand,
Yes, I can smile again.

Blessed in cities.
Blessed is the fruit of my body.
Blessed is my basket.
I am blessed as I come and go.

And no matter how winds may blow through the windows,
exposing the glow of the moon,

I can smile again,
for I know
My Heavenly Father
watches over me

Songs of praise stomp down the shadows
It kicks out the unwanted feelings of regret.

Aloud, are the timbral
Aloud, are the voices.

Clapping hands, dancing tears,
give my shame and burdens a different rhythm

Joy comes in morning lights
Sorrows do turn into gladness
And God cheers with His infinite pleasure.

Yes, the tears have soaked my pillow.
Holding me down as I felt inconsolable.
but with the past behind me, on a different day.
In a new season.
Transformed.
Renewed.

With Jesus refreshing love, I can smile again, for
in the streets, in the cities, I am blessed.

YOUR SONG

Yes, the tears have soaked my pillow, Yes, I lived an old life.
I was held down for a long time.
But now I Can smile again because I am blessed

I Felt such burdens, couldn't figure things out.
I fought battles and wanted to give up.
Found by your perfect love, you rescued me so.
Of my new chorus, I can smile again because I am blessed.

Yes, Yes, Oh Lord, I am blessed.

Reflection

On account of good and bad times, there are certain situations that can make you smile. Not only smile but laugh, feel cheery and simply glad, and yes, it can last just as long as a bad time. Those who study and understand how the body works, will tell you that smiling does release certain chemicals in your body. From *Psychology Today*, guest blogger Sarah Stevenson describes that "smiling activates the release of neuropeptides that work toward fighting off stress."[1] She goes further on to explain that "They facilitate messaging to the whole body when we are happy, sad, angry, depressed, or excited. The feel-good neurotransmitters—dopamine, endorphins and serotonin—are all released when a smile flashes across your face as well."[2] Relative to the feelings of joy, happiness is usually experienced when you are satisfied, content, and at peace for what has and will happen. For some people, smiling can come easy, while for others, it hurts too much. It is without a doubt that you will not feel happy all the time. There are days when the hardships of life will inflict you. You will try to at least grin through it and hope for the best. But despite the difficulties, you eventually gain a reason to smile because deep down, something on the inside gives hope.

When you have lost your smile, and find it again,
that within itself is a blessing. It is a miracle.

The children of Israel, who had been in slavery for 400 years, certainly understood what it meant to lose their smile. They had been oppressed and used by the Egyptians to build a great city that was not their own. Following the ten plagues, the day finally came, when the great IAM, performed one of the greatest miracles ever done in history.

Following the instructions of the Lord, *"...Moses stretched out his hand over the sea; and the Lord caused the sea to go back by a strong east wind all that night, and made the sea dry land, and the waters were divided. And the children*

---

of Israel went into the midst of the sea upon the dry ground: and the waters were a wall unto them on their right hand, and on their left" (Exodus 14:21-22). Following this event, it was a joyous occasion. Moses and the children of Israel regained their smile in song.: *"...I will sing unto the Lord, for he hath triumphed gloriously: the horse and his rider hath he thrown into the sea. The Lord is my strength and song, and he is become my salvation: he is my God, and I will prepare him an habitation; my father's God, and I will exalt him"* (Exodus 15: 1-2).

Of the many things you can go through, and experience within a lifetime, when you are compelled to smile again, like the children of Israel, there are no words to describe how that really feels. It is like when you have been carrying a load for so long - for years - and finally, The Lord comes and says, *"Arise, this is a new day for you. The Pharaoh you have seen yesterday, you shall see no more. The sins of your past are wiped clean. Come, walk in this new life."*

When you hear such words, it is then you come to know and understand how blessed you are. You will accept the peace to know that the problems of yesterday and today are of no consequence. You can smile again as you move forward on dry land.

A true statement, from the poetical proverb proclaims,
"The blessing of the Lord, it maketh rich, and he
addeth no sorrow with it." (Proverbs 10:22)

As it is encouraged, when you harken (listen) to the instructions of God, (like Moses stretching out his rod), you are guaranteed to receive the blessings He will give (perform) unto you. You will be *"blessed"* when you go and *"blessed when [you] come in"*

When situations turn around for your good, and the tears have stopped, you have every right to shout and sing. Like David, you can say, *"This is the Lord's doing; it is marvellous in our eyes. This is the day which the Lord hath made; we will rejoice and be glad in it"* (Psalm 118: 23-24).

With Jesus refreshing love.
[you] can smile again, in the streets, in the cities, for [you are] blessed.

TODAY YOU CAN SING THE LORD SONG "I CAN
SMILE AGAIN BECAUSE I AM BLESSED."

Scripture Reference
Deuteronomy ♦ Revelations 7:16-17 ♦ Matthew 5:6

Your Day's Reflection

_____

_____

_____

_____

_____

_____

_____

_____

_____

Pursue, Overtake, Recover ALL

*And David enquired at the LORD, saying, Shall I pursue after
this troop? Shall I overtake them? And he answered him, Pursue:
for thou shalt surely overtake them, and without fail recover all*
♦ 1 Samuel 30:8

*Let the redeemed of the Lord say so, whom he hath
redeemed from the hand of the enemy;*
♦ Psalms 107:2

*He sent redemption unto his people: he hath commanded his covenant
forever: holy and reverend is his name.* **♦ Psalms 111:9**

THE VERSE

Multitudes of sands and seas
buried my hope to the depth of impossibility.

The sun in its array ran away.
Dreadful hands reached the shore,
and reached precious stones.

Piercing eyes bored us whole,
with the stolen glory hidden away.
The enemy snarled and gnarled my soul to stow away.
He laughed and scorned us

for being God's children.

Then...

The songs on Hills winged down the clouds with a sound.
It was a sound coming from the essence of souls found

With my sword swift with the wind,
like a warrior, I chop down the dead tree.

I chop down the reminders of the old past.
I chop down erected mockeries of my stains and sins.

For the blessings of redemption,
I open my heart to be free.

Retribution stomping through the ages,
with voices, raised high
and eyes cast upon the prize.
Victory ahead, I stand up straight.

I stand up tall.
I stand firm and proclaim,
that which the devil stole from me
I go with the Lords permission
to pursue, overtake and recover all.

With the double edge sword,
I hold nothing back.
Holding up the banner of triumph,
My peace restored with joy,
I recover my children with my family.
My joy restored with gladness
I recover my home with prosperity.

But most of all

I Want to Sing Your Song

I recover my soul.

Standing straight,
standing tall
I shout the proclamation:
That which the devil stole,
I with the Lord's permission,
pursue, overtake and recover it all.

YOUR SONG

I Pursue Joy
I Pursue Happiness
I Pursue Love
From you God

I Pursue strength
I Pursue righteousness
I Pursue peace
From you…Jesus
I recover it all
I recover it all
I recover it all
I recover it all

Reflection

Can you remember the last time you had something or someone of great significance taken from you? It wasn't just taken, it was stolen. To make matters worse, the way it was done not only left you in tears, but it also left you in shambles. It left you struggling to pick up the pieces of your troubled mind, and it took you a great while before you could recover.

Stealing, thievery, and robbery in and of itself is a terrible offence. It can make anyone feel exposed, vulnerable and like a fool. But what makes it that much worse is the devastation that follows after the act has been committed. When you are robbed, no matter how little the object maybe, it is never easy to just accept that it happened. Especially when that which is taken is next to impossible to replace. Categorically, anything or even anyone can be taken from us. It could be a valuable object that is replaceable, or tragically enough, a person who is not replaceable. Apart from an object or a person, other valuables can be equally hard to replace and or recover. It could be your peace of mind, your identity, or your sense of value. With malicious intent, people can employ manipulative means to take anything away from you. They can even make you believe that you don't deserve to be here.

The unveiling of history reveal that at the hands of human slavery, trafficking, and cultural assimilation, there have been races and nationalities of people, who have been robbed of their sense of identity, freedom, and the right to be human. This has led to deep scars and wounds, which despite the efforts towards healing and reconciliation, the damage seems next to irreparable.

But, when something is taken from you, there is an instinctive reaction to go after what belongs to you. Reason being, it is never easy to live with the thought that this person I love; this possession I hold dear, is lost to me forever.

**There does come a time
when that which has been lost/stolen can be recovered.**

Redemption, which is a word associated with recovery, is enacted when a possession has been stolen or taken. Within the accounts of biblical history, the central underlining theme points to the redemption of God's people. In the Complete Jewish translation, it identifies how *"By God's grace, [we] were once slaves to sin [obeying from our hearts] the pattern of teaching to which [we] were exposed;"* (Romans (Rom) 6:17 ᶜᴶᴮ).

The narratives of the people from time past, which are interconnected, from page to page, demonstrate God's wondrous works of victory and deliverance. Celebrated and recognized as salvation, the redemption, Jesus wrought on the cross, paves the way for those lost in sin to be saved.

During the time of David being king over Israel, he had to face the consequence of Saul's previous disobedience. At the hands of the Amalekites, David's family was kidnapped, and his home was burnt to the ground. The people were so bitter with sorrow they wept until they could cry no more. Angry, they sought to stone David.

In turn, he enquired of the LORD, *"Shall I pursue after this troop? Shall I overtake them?"*

God replied saying, *"Pursue: for thou shalt surely overtake them, and without fail recover all"* (1 Samuel 30:8).

To receive such a response, it surely kindled a fire in David, especially since he had God's permission. This meant he was guaranteed to win the battle and reclaim back what his enemies stole.

Fast-forwarding to that moment as the story goes:

"... David recovered all that the Amalekites had carried away: and David rescued his two wives. And there was nothing lacking to them, neither small nor great, neither sons nor daughters, neither spoil, nor any thing that they had taken to them: ..." (1 Samuel 30: 17-18)

Looking back over your life, and where you have been, what has your enemy stolen from you? Is it your peace of mind? Your voice to speak? Has the enemy invaded your home and kidnapped your spouse and children? Has your joy been plundered?

While there are some things you cannot get back, there are some possessions you have the permission to *"pursue, overtake and recover."* Best

---

of all, you are not alone in your pursuit, you have the Lord on your side who is "a *man of war...*" (Ex 15:3a).

He goes before you to fight your battles and
grants you the victory to overcome.

With your sword swift with the wind,
like a warrior...
[you] *can pursue, reclaim and recover all which*
the enemy of [your] *soul as stolen*

TODAY YOU CAN SING THE LORD'S SONG. "I PURSUE JOY,
I PURSUE HAPPINESS, I PURSUE LOVE"

Scripture Reference
1 Samuel 30:8;17-18 ♦ Psalm 107:2 ♦ Psalm 111:9 ♦ Exodus 15:3

I Want to Sing Your Song

Your Day's Reflection

_____

_____

_____

_____

_____

_____

_____

_____

_____

The Whole Armour of God

Finally, my brethren, be strong in the Lord, and in the power of his might.
Put on the whole armour of God, that ye may be
able to stand against the wiles of the devil...
♦ **1 Ephesians 6:11-10**

Be sober, be vigilant; because your adversary the devil, as a
roaring lion, walketh about, seeking whom he may devour:
♦ **1 Peter 5:8**

THE VERSE

The Lord strong and mighty is my strength.
To withstand against the wiles of wickedness,
there is an armour of God that protects and shields me.

In the secret place of the Most-High,
under His shadows, I shall abide.
Sober enough,
I will be able to see the deception
in the gatherings of perverse smiles.

My seat will not be found in the council of the corrupt.

Covered beneath the Lord's shadow,
His truth shall be my shield and buckler.

Having on the breastplate of righteousness
My heart is protected from the flying arrows.

Roaring about is the lion seeking womb he may devour.
Adorn in skin seemingly pure
He speaks motivation so sweet,
yet there is a deadly venom
to contaminate the purity of imaginations.

The desires in one heart can multiply
into a multitude of one burden.
The weight of it can stoop the knees
to succumb to the lust of delicate,
yet pretentious words.
In the lies, there is a prison
which seeks to keep the soul captive.

My feet shod with the preparation of the gospel of peace,
and with the shield of faith,
I can quench all the fiery darts,
changing into different shape-shifting forms.

The pestilence that walketh in darkness
Destruction wasting at noonday.
By thousands, they shall fall and not come nigh.

Therefore, upon my head, the helmet of salvation guards my zeal.

Wielding the sword of the Spirit,
it is my weapon to combat the principalities in high places.
mighty they are to the pulling down of strongholds.

Carefully, strategically, wisely
with the precision of prayers, the battle is won.
Having done all,
I stand with my *loins girt about with truth.*

YOUR SONG

Put on the armour of Jesus Christ
Put on the armour of Jesus Christ,
For there are powers to fight.
Powers to fight
No wrestling against the flesh and blood.
For their powers to fight.

Shod with the gospel of peace
Taking on the shield of faith,

I must put on the armour of Christ
Put on the armour of Jesus Christ

With the helmet of salvation, and swift with the sword of the spirit.
Having done all, I stand.
Putting on the armour of Jesus Christ

Reflection

Going to war is no easy feat, and without the proper gear, the battle and can turn from bad to worse. Intense, there are combats for which certain weapons can cause fatal damage to the body. Even if a person is strong enough, and is skilled in hand to hand combat, without the proper armour, the end results can be detrimental.

For any type of battle or combative situation, there are "rules of engagement"[1], and strategies which guide groups of combatants on how to fight. With rules of engagement, there are specific limitations that direct a solider on how to engage their enemies. Strategies which are employed in combat are methods which ensures there will be victory. It considers all the possible areas where an enemy can be taken down.

Fighting without the fortitude of the right weapons, and gears is quite dangerous. Fighting without your mental fortitude intact can be deadly. Some weapons are not physically lethal but are just as deadly.

Christians which are in a warfare against spiritual wickedness in high places, do have a strategy that is effective in battle. Detailed in the account of Ephesians, provided is an armour that ALL believers are implored to wear.

"[gird] your waist with truth... put on the breastplate of righteousness.... shod your feet with the preparation of the gospel of peace...[have] on the shield of faith with which you will be able to quench all the fiery darts of the wicked one. And take the helmet of salvation and the sword of the Spirit, which is the word of God; praying always with all prayer and supplication in the Spirit, being watchful to this end with all perseverance and supplication for all the saints" (Ephesians 6:10,11a, 12-14).

It is without a doubt that in the natural order of things there are human to human combats. As it would be manifested in the physical, you could be dealing with an enemy like a Peninnah, Goliath or the Amalekites, but the real battle and strategy is spiritual.

Peter, one of the commissioned disciples, had his experience of encountering the "wiles" of the devil. Trained by the Chief Cornerstone (Jesus), he understood, that the battle was only won by prayer and fasting (Matt 17:21).

Addressing the brethren, he gives this warning. *"Stay sober, stay alert! Your enemy, the Adversary, stalks about like a roaring lion looking for someone to devour. Stand against him, firm in your trust, knowing that your brothers throughout the world are going through the same kinds of suffering"* (1 Kefa (1 Pe) 5:8-9 CJB).

So as the armour is important to put on, it is critical that the person wearing the armour is sober. The rules of engagement for any child of God, is to understand:

"For though we walk in the flesh, we do not war after the flesh: For the weapons of our warfare are not carnal, but mighty through God to the pulling down of strong holds;" (2 Corinthians 10:3-4).

"Carefully, strategically, wisely with precision of prayers the battle is won. Having done all, [you] stand with [your] loins girt about with truth.

TODAY YOU CAN SING THE LORD SONG OF STRATEGY
"PUT ON THE ARMOUR OF JESUS CHRIST"

Scripture Reference
Ephesians 6:10,11a,12-14 ♦ 1 Peter 5:8 ♦ 2 Corinthians 10: 3-4

I Want to Sing Your Song

Your Day's Reflection

Don't Want to be Afraid

Thou shalt not be afraid for the terror by night; nor for the arrow that flieth by day; Nor for the pestilence that walketh in darkness; nor for the destruction that wasteth at noonday.
♦ **Psalms 91:5-6**

For God hath not given us the spirit of fear; but of power, and of love, and of a sound mind.
♦ *2 Timothy 1:7*

THE VERSE

I won't be afraid no more.
I will be assured.
I will step out on faith and believe Him, my hope of Glory.

When voices threaten to take away and destroy.
Jezebel's spirit stands tall,
a stubborn pillar intimidating even the mighty of men.
This one thing is forever true.
God hath not given me the spirit of fear,
therefore, I will not run in haste. I will not be afraid

If God be for me, why should I fret
If demons tremble at the name of Jesus

Which is sweeter to me than silken honey
Why should I hide at the sounds of horsemen coming?
Why should I shroud under the pressure of thoughts
which presume I won't make it.

No! I cannot let this fear cripple me,
Then, I cannot move towards my destiny.
No! I cannot live my life on the wayside
as if my one life does not matter.
No! I cannot let fear cause my faith to wane.

If God be for me,
why should I be afraid of the terror by night?
If He is my fortress,
why let arrows,
pestilence, and destruction
dictate my every move.

The Lord does not slumber,
nor does He sleep.
Therefore, I shall not be disturbed.
I shall not be moved.
My sleep shall be sweet.
My mind shall be at peace and not tossed about.

No! I will not be afraid anymore.
I will rest assured of the Lord's promise.
On the steps of faith I climb up
to the highest peaks of confidence.
I walk on water towards my Saviour,
who gives me the authority to "*Come.*"

Even though swarms of "terrors."
fly around like swarms of vultures taunting the flesh,
the Lord of Host has given his angels charge to encamp.

With one foot in front of the other,
I walk on the platform of prosperity.
The Lord is my Keeper,
the Lord is my shade upon my right hand.

My face may press against the grain of expectation,
and my might body decay from the pestilence of mortality,
But I will not be afraid.
I will be assured of the promise.
I will step out on faith and believe.
For God has not given me the spirit of fear
but of power, love and a sound mind.

Your Song

I won't be afraid no more (No-o)
I will be assured (in the promises)
I will step out on faith and believe you
In the promises that you said to me (yeah)

I don't want to be afraid, I don't want to
I don't want to be afraid, I don't want to

I can't let fear get a hold of me (No-o)
When it's your face I see.
I want to step on the water, and believe
Can keep going to my liberty

I don't want to be afraid; I don't want to (I
don't want to be afraid no more)
I don't want to be afraid, I don't want to

Reflection

What are you afraid of? What is your biggest fear? These are the kind of questions most of us struggle to face, when we have to confront the fear or truth of the whole matter. Usually, when you are afraid, the concern is fed by the uncomfortable sensation you would feel when challenged by what you don't know or understand. And even if you do understand your fear mingles with the perception of a terrible outcome. For example: if an awful monster were to come in your house, your instincts would kick in, and your thoughts would race to the conclusion that this *monster will shred me to pieces.*

In war, fear is a part of the strategy which opposing forces use to expose the weak areas. Intimidation, which is apart of such tactics, is often initiated to cause opposing forces to lose confidence and focus. When this happens, vulnerable areas are exposed, which gives the enemy an opportunity to attack.

For Gods people, who are caught in the war between Good and Evil, one of the many devices that is used against us, is fear.

Elijah, who was a great prophet, was empowered to do great exploits for God. He stood up against the Baal prophets, who carried out evil administrations against Gods people, to worship a false deity. By calling fire down from heaven, Elijah showed the children of Israel, that God was real. With boldness and authority, he ordered the prophets of Baal to be slain. Despite the power he displayed, Jezebel, the evil queen of Israel sent a menacing messaging:

"May the gods do terrible things to me and worse ones besides if by this time tomorrow I haven't taken your life, just as you took theirs!" (M'lakhim Alef (1 Ki) 19:2 ᶜᴶᴮ).

Elijah when he received the message, ran for his life and hid under a juniper tree. He prayed for his life to be taken, and such a request signified how terrified he was. While Elijah was hiding, the Lord ministered to him. He showed the despondent Elijah three demonstrations of: a strong wind, earthquake, and fire.

In the midst of all these, there was a still small voice. But as anyone would ask why was God showing Elijah this demonstration? How was it suppose to help him?

Well in essence, Jezebel had been loud, with her killing of the Lord's prophets (1 King 19:11-3). So, one could say the powerful displays signified that God is not in the noise of taking care of matters. However, when the time comes, He will do things in the open for His purpose and glory. Of His own "strategic" method, God directed Elijah to replace Ahab. As for Jezebel, it was Eunuchs who threw her out of her own window (2 Kings 9:30).

Sometimes, when you face real threats that terrorize your life, it can be scary. But in the book of 2 Timothy 1:7, Paul reminds us

"For God has not given us a spirit of fear, but of power and of love and of a sound mind."

With one foot in front of the other,
[you can] *walk on the platform of prosperity.*
The Lord is [your] *Keeper*

TODAY, YOU CAN SING THE LORD'S SONG "I
WON'T WANT BE AFRAID NO MORE"

Scripture Reference
1 Kings 20, 19 ♦ Psalms 91: 5-6 ♦ 2 Timothy 1:7

Your Day's Reflection

You Are My Strength

*I can do all things through Christ which
strengtheneth me.* ◆ **Philippians 4:13**

*He giveth power to the faint; and to them that have no might he increaseth
strength. Even the youths shall faint and be weary, and the young men
shall utterly fall: But they that wait upon the Lord shall renew their
strength; they shall mount up with wings as eagles; they shall run, and
not be weary; and they shall walk, and not faint.* ◆ **Isaiah 40:29-31**

THE VERSE

On this new day, as the morning arises,
I swing my feet over the side of a resting place.
I lift my head and brace my shoulder for the day I must face.

Far out, some things are not that clear.
Obscurity often shades my eyes from seeing
that which is right,
so I 'am likely to make mistakes and go in the wrong way.

On this new day
as roads and cultures change.
Around corners of crossroads,
nothing is guaranteed to be that easy.
But looking to You the Author of my race,

I Want to Sing Your Song

I see Your face and know
I can do all things through You who
strengthen me.

Waiting on You is the wisest thing I could ever do.
For you, see the future and know what is to come.
You know what is the best outcome.

On the up climb of sloops and steeps,
there are jagged edges stones which do cut to the bone.
Some troubles will encompass about.
There are weights which do easily beset.
For life is not a straight way,
for there are combinations of joy and dismay.

Your hands, Oh Lord, are what I need
to give me the touch of vision and clarity.

When my heart is overwhelmed by loads of cares,
it is sometimes difficult to speak it out loud.

While I struggle to let go,
and forgive the hardest of matters,
it is your strength for which I beseech.

Through the process of change,
somethings will not stay the same.
My assurance is knowing.
Your Word will sustain.

You are my strength of the morning.
You are my strength of the moonlight.
Weary and worn from battles fought with a vengeance,
it is your healing palms that mend the broken fences.

If not for any other day,

Lord of the fathers,
and children, come what may,
all I need in the heat of moments is
Your grace to live.

In the absence of temperance, you support.
In the absence of self-control, you enclose.
In the absence of vision, you are my eyes.
In the presence of weakness, you are my strength.

YOUR SONG

You are my strength when I am weak
You are my strength when I am worn
And when I feel like I can't go on
You are my strength and you are strong

Life sometimes feels like a whirlwind
Tumbling everything around me.

Reflection

I WILL SING OF THY STRENGTH
You are my strength when I am weak.
You are my strength when I am worn.

Fear, which has been established as an element of power and control, can cause you to feel intimidated, weak, and hopeless. The reason being, the things you fear illuminates the vision of things not turning around for your good. While it does take a process to overcome it, you can do so when you have the support of strength and confidence to do so.

Strength, which is needed every day, is the quality and state to brace against opposing pressures.[1] It might not be an opposition of conflict, where someone is fighting you, but it could be pressure from the tasks or burdens you have to deal with consistently. As your strength will wane, from time to time, there is a resiliency produced through the survival of your social development. This is known as problem-solving skills and coping mechanisms, which you can learn over time. In your natural capacity to deal with problems as they arise, there will be an undoubted willpower to push through. Somehow, whether you realize it or not, your mind, which is central to your instincts, will activate your resistance to brace up. In the heat of the moment, you learn just how strong you are.

In the silence and quietest of places you do find
solace to reset your mind, and gain strength.

With the variety of elements that can drain your energy, there is also the inner self that can be equally challenging. Within the self, you have your heart, mind, spirit, and soul, which harness the emotions that change from one state to another. For example, it is a common and universal theory that there is *a thin line between love and hate.*[2] The struggle resides in the emotions which waver between temperance and lack of self-control.

Samson, who was a man of impeccable strength, had his enemies to deal with, but the one he was not prepared for was Delilah. Sadly, and quite tragically, his mind was not sober enough to recognize the strategy his real enemies were using against him in the form of a woman (Judges 16). This account signified that the inner strength does not always involve the use of lethal weapons, but it does require the stamina of the mind to be vigilant and sober (1 Peter 5:8).

Varying by degrees, there are times when you can manage to get by with the strength already given. This would be your willpower, determination, and conscious effort to push through. There is absolutely nothing wrong in relying on your own strength because God made you to be strong and powerful. The only difference is, in your humanness, it is not enough.

When your strength decreases the Lord will "...[*give*] *power to the faint; and to them that have no might he increaseth strength. Even the youths shall faint and be weary, and the young men shall utterly fall: But they that wait upon the Lord shall renew their strength; they shall mount up with wings as eagles; they shall run, and not be weary; and they shall walk, and not faint*" (Isaiah 40:29-31).

Throughout the seasons of your life, there will be countless occurrences for which you will need a boost. Jesus does not expect his people to be perfect all the time. He more than understands that you will get weak and tired. From this observation, He recognized that "*The spirit indeed is willing, but the flesh is weak,*" So he encourages "*Watch and pray, lest you enter into temptation*" (Matthew 26:41).

Even though Samson woefully lost his anointed strength, he still got it back and was able to do more damage than when he was vibrant.

You might be feeling low, tired, and scared but it is okay, you "... *can do all things through Christ which strengtheneth* [you]" (Philippians 4:13).

In the absence of temperance, [Jesus] sustains
In the absence of self-control, [Yahweh] encloses
In the absence of vision, [Jehovah] becomes the eyes
In the presence of weakness, [God is your strength]

TODAY YOU CAN SING THE LORD'S SONG: "YOU
ARE MY STRENGTH WHEN I AM WEAK"

Scripture Reference
Judges 16 ♦ Isaiah 40:29-31 ♦ Philippians 4:13 ♦ Matthew 26:41

Your Day's Reflection

_____

_____

_____

_____

_____

_____

_____

_____

_____

We Have the Power, We have the Victory

Behold, I give unto you power to tread on serpents and scorpions,
and over all the power of the enemy: and nothing
shall by any means hurt you. ♦ **Luke 10:19**

"Yet in all these things we are more than conquerors
through Him who loved us." ♦ **Romans 8:37**

"And the angel of the Lord appeared unto him, and said unto him,
The Lord is with thee, thou mighty" man of valour. ♦ **Judges 6:12**

THE VERSE

Why should I give up and cry?
Why should I weep, and I hide?
When I have found the virtue and valor,
I have found the weapon and triumph.

Thinking I would never find it,
I thought the battle would overtake and I would lose.
Now I know it is not so, because love came and rescued me.

A new creature created in the image of Christ.
Upon serpents and scorpions,

I tread for they cannot determine my end.

The willpower to live is my right.
I am a child of God,
given the boldness to come boldly to the throne of grace.
God gave Christ as the lamb, who is my hope of glory.

A fountain with rivers that never run dry,
He gave me the cup of redemption
for me to drink and be revived.

Why oh, why should I sin?
Why should I be angry
when the Lord has made me glad
for continuous days of new mornings?

With Jesus name, I have found the way
I have found another chance.
I have found myself a new salvation plan.

In the woods of tall trees, where paths are hidden,
I hear the call of the Father telling me
"Use that which is in your hand."

In my mouth, like a furnace of the tongue,
I speak the authority.

I have the power; I have the victory.

I have the power to dance.
I have victory to sing.
I have the weapon to wield.
I have the empowered shield.

I do not have to hide under a tree.
I do not have to run away

because the devil makes be believe
I don't have much long to last.

Speaking it so, I give the victory cry.
I denounce the existences of evil altars.
I pronounce the blessing of my soul to
prosper.
I denounce the pestilence creeping in walls to overtake.

I proclaim the success of my hands to embrace.
I affirm the Lords will in my life to be done.

Raising the flag of triumph and song,
high above my head, I wave it well
for I have been forgiven of my wrongs.

Yesterday is a report I have yet to tell.
Contrarily, today is written in the Lord's mouth
and spoken on prayers.

The Holy Spirit stirs and creates the motion.

Of the gift of discernment,
that which is hidden
is revealed for reassurance and endurance.

If God be for me, who shall be against me.
I have the power to dance, and
I have victory to sing.

I have the weapon to wield, and
I have the shield to withstand.

I have the power; I have the victory

YOUR SONG

I found grace joy and happiness within,
since I took upon, upon my Saviour's names
Yeah, the Lord is with me
I shall fear no evil
We have the power we have the victory

We have the power
We have the victory
We have the power
We have the victory
If God is for us, then who can be against us
We have the power we have the victory

We are more than conquers since Jesus came and died on Calvary
No weapon formed against me
Shall prosper
We have the power
We have the victory

Reflection

The experience of victory, over a long drawn out battle, is an extreme vigorous sensation that is beyond explanation. The motions of profound joy rush through the body, along with the bittersweet realization that the war is over. For anyone to truly understand what victory means, one would have to step into the shoes of soldier. The world as you will know it today, is underline with the scars of war. The events of World 1 and 2, significantly impacted a lot of people's lives. Respectably on Remembrance Day (November 11), a moment of silence is given to honour those who have fought and died. Poppy flowers are worn to symbolize the pain, sorrow, and sacrifice men and women have suffered. While such loss is never easy to process, the beauty of victory gives the strength to know life is honourable when you live on.

For the gospel of Christ, there have been those
who have fought the good fight of faith.
(2 Timothy (2 Ti) 4:7a [CJB]**)**

In Christendom, there have been faithful soldiers, and warriors of God's army, who have committed themselves to the cause of winning souls for Christ.

In the True Report of "great strategy" it is reassured

"Behold, I give unto you power to tread on serpents and scorpions, and over all the power of the enemy: and nothing shall by any means hurt you."

But it is also stipulated, *"rejoice not, that the spirits are subject unto you; but rather rejoice, because your names are written in heaven"* (Luke 10:19-20).

In other words, the greatest prize of all spiritual battles is knowing your prize – being your name – is written in the lamb's book of life.

In the book of Romans, it is declared *"In all these things we are more than conquerors through him that loved us."* (Romans 8:37).

As children of the King, Jesus has not left you to fend on your own. The Lord who is your battle axe and mighty in battle has given you the power to be victorious over every situation. When you know you have the power, and you know the battle is won, before it starts, fear will have no dominion over you. You will forge ahead singing *"I have the victory."* What is even sweeter is when the enemy thinks he has won, and God allows him to think like this because there is a *Special weapon*, you have which the devil cannot see, or destroy, and that is the power of God living in you. Surely, you might feel like Gideon, overwhelmed and want to shroud yourself into the shadows. You are troubled on every side; bombs are thrown at you and there is no time to barely duck. But God reminds in His word that *there is no weapon that is form against you that shall prosper* (Isaiah 54:17).

This Power, when you know that you have it, sends a great charge through the body. Fear, worry, and stress are the least of emotions that will bother you. Even when the enemy will try to intimidate you, once you know that you got it, there is no stopping you.

With the power on [your] *tongue… speak it here; speak*
it now…I have the power…I have the victory

TODAY YOU CAN SING THE LORD'S SONG "I HAVE
THE POWER; I HAVE THE VICTORY"

Scripture Reference
Luke 10:19 ♦ Romans 8:37 ♦ Psalms 23:4

I Want to Sing Your Song

Your Day's Reflection

_____

_____

_____

_____

_____

_____

_____

_____

_____

Part 1: Called to Purpose

For we are His workmanship, created in Christ Jesus unto good works, which God hath before ordained that we should walk in them ♦ **Ephesians 2:10**

And we know that all things work together for good to those who love God, to those who are the called according to His purpose.
♦ **Romans 8:28** NKJV

THE VERSE

Arrayed on platters of streets, and city lights,
I 'am illuminated for eyes to see.

In the way, I walk with the voice
carrying the wisdom of my testimony.
It is the song of how you saved.
It is the melody of how you loved.
It is the chorus of how you lifted.

When death came knocking,
through the prayers of saints,
you took my heart with the gaping hole and mended it whole.

Breathing and thumping with the blood you blessed,
I am here because you gave this soul a purpose,
a mission to see to the end.

There is a reason why I am still here and alive.
There is a reason why I am here, and for that, I feel blessed.

Interlaced with the call of seasons,
there is a distinct sound that flourishes.

Like a cloud of smoke,
it threads in the morrow of my bones.
Waking me up at will,
it pounds in my head, and I can't help but see multiple visions.

I know the success. I see the victory.

In dreams of countless nights,
I see the youth: men and women, writing letters for their misery.
I hear the songs of Levites played on pianos keys.
I see the shepherds of flocks standing on pulpits,
their voice is thunderous of Your coming.

In the wake of sunrises,
I hear the agony of many,
waiting for me to sing heavens harmony.
Waiting is what they do
because they need me to tell them the truth of Emmanuel's name.

In the realm, for which only the spirit knows,
I hear the weeping of souls
waiting for me to tell them to come home.

Some are caught at crossroads,
seeking, looking and not sure
that Your tabernacles is the house of bread, available for all to come in.

A light for those imprisoned,
a might of strength, for the weary placed in graves forgotten.
It is your commission, which gives me permission to go and get them.

In the halls of liberty,
I become the inspiration with wings spreading far out.
Withholding nothing, the purpose has become my *verse and song.*

A destiny that cannot be denied,
I am the fisher of men,
abounding on the path of high-rise waves.
Riding them, I absorb the power,
as I propel forward.
I must reach the feet standing on sands.

In the womb of Heavenly wisdom, and God's image,
is the children of men waiting to be fed.
The legacy contained in elders' hand,
is the power to be passed down to generation after.

Between the mix, is the purpose
ready to be written on mankind's affirmations.

Created for your glory.
Created for your honour.
Amongst the call, I am chosen.
No matter the cost, I know, Oh Lord, I must get this done.

YOUR SONG

I was created for Your glory
I was created for your honour
To be the light and exalt Your Holy Name

You have chosen me to be a witness,
To be all that You called me to be.
My life is in Your hands, all according to Your plan.
You chose Me.

Reflection

I WILL SING FOR THE CAUSE...FOR THE PURPOSE
Jesus will call, and I will answer.

Have you ever felt a tug; a pull for which you cannot describe? Like a soft whisper, it carols like a hum in your spirit, and it tickles your resolve to arise and push ahead. Stirring in your soul, you feel the questions and as you process through the weight of it, you can feel the impression on your heart. Try as you might, you can no longer ignore it. In your dreams, you can see it. In your waking hours, you can feel it. You keep hearing a song in your spirit, and the lyrics tumble out your mouth on a melody. *It's not the only one.* Immediately after you have finish writing the first one, more keeps coming.

Later down the road following a harrowing experience you are standing before a group of people, sharing how you have come out of it. You find yourself pursing that tug as you persevere through your academics and professional endeavors. From specific interactions with other people, something in you comes alive. You see a hungry man on the street, and unlike those who do see him, and do give him money, something in you says *"Go, he needs more than food. He needs help."* And all you can think to do is jump full steam ahead.

By its defining nature, purpose gives meaning to your existence, and every single person is born with it. It underscores the wisdom for you to know your life is not a waste, and there is a divine reason as to why only you can hear that song. Why only you can hear voices crying for help. It might take you a while to discover it is there, and that is okay. Eventually, the call gets loud enough for you to hear, and it only becomes a matter of time. From the account of Ecclesiastes, it gives the founding principal that *there is a reason and a purpose for every living creature under the sun* (Ecclesiastes 3). It virtually answers the questions that you might ask yourself when you encounter or experience a defining moment.

Purpose will call to you at any time.

Joshua, who came from the seed of promise, shared his dreams, and for the rest of his life, it led to him being the saviour for his people who experienced a drought (Joshua 37). David use to tend to sheep, not knowing that a man named Samuel would come to His house to anoint him to be King of the Jews (1 Samuel 16). Esther probably didn't think she attend a ball and become a queen; *a strategic* move by God to save the Hebrews from genocide (Esther 4:14).

The account of Jeremiah also demonstrates that when you were being formed in your mother's womb, God had (and still has) a purpose and a plan for you (Jeremiah 1:5). It is not separate from anything you do unless it is out of the will of God. As written,

"We are His workmanship, created in Christ Jesus unto good works, which God hath before ordained that we should walk in them." (Ephesians 2:10).

Created for [His] *glory*
Designed for…honour, amongst the call, You are chosen…

TODAY, YOU ARE CALLED TO SING THE LORD'S SONG: "I WAS CREATED FOR YOUR GLORY I WAS CREATED FOR YOUR HONOUR"

Scripture Reference
Ephesians 2:10 ♦ Jeremiah 29:11 ♦ Romans 8:28 ♦ Ecclesiastes 3

Your Day's Reflection

Part 2: The Gift of Ministry

And God has appointed these in the church: first apostles, second prophets, third teachers, after that miracles, then gifts of healings, helps, administrations, varieties of tongues. ♦ **I Corinthians 12:28** NKJV

And He Himself gave some to be apostles, some prophets, some evangelists, and some pastors and teachers, for the equipping of the saints for the work of ministry, for the edifying of the body of Christ,
♦ **Ephesians 4:11-12** NKJV

So, we being many, are one body in Christ, and individually members of one another. Having then gifts differing according to the grace that is given to us, let us use them: if prophecy, let us prophesy in proportion to our faith; or ministry, let us use it in our ministering; he who teaches, in teaching; he who exhorts, in exhortation; he who gives, with liberality; he who leads, with diligence; he who shows mercy, with cheerfulness. ♦ **Romans 12:5-8** NKJV

THE VERSE

From the washing of our soul to the rebirth
transformed, we are the vessel empowered
to do the Lord's bidding in the realms of the earth.

New hands and feet,
we march for the Kingdom,
embarking upon the pilgrim's journey.

I Want to Sing Your Song

Draped in Yahwey's will,
we fight for the suppress and oppressed.

When we are unified,
there is an explosion of an expanding cloud
in the gathering of gifted praise.

On one accord of belief and mission,
the gift of the Holy Ghost is poured unto all flesh.
A mystery for angels to guide,
it is the edification for the bride of Christ.

A ministry for salvation,
the doctrine is to preach
in the highways and byways
where those lost can find the throne of atonement.

Without asking, we are the chosen generation.
Given a touch of great divinity, we need no unwrapping.

Unveiled through mysteries of deep inward longings,
the purpose illuminates the gift in the mouth.

A disciple called out from among them.
It is a commitment to the task.
showing forth the greatness of God's unmerited favour.

The gift of ministry no man can give
We are called the apostles for the Lord's word.
Speak it, we must.
We are called the teachers,
to exemplify and magnify
the inspiration and liberation of truth.

We are called the evangelist to tend to the father's sheep.
We are called the hands of miracles

to wrought the healing of deliverance
for those broken from inflictions.

We being many are of the one body,
for in Christ, we are the children of the highest,
called to the task.

Empowered with the gift to edify the body,
and glorify the Lord,
in the bond of peace
we are the ministry of Gifts for reconciliation.

YOUR SONG

In one accord we are strong
In one message we speak the same

created for Your glory
created for your honour
we are the chosen, called to the great commission
from your permission
we can go with gift to get them.

Reflection

I WILL SING THE SONG OF MINISTRY
I Was Created for The Great Commission

Liken to a kingdom, organizations are formed of people who function to carry out specified operations. Categorized into departments of skills and talent, members within the organization will be tasked with different responsibilities. Each department supports the company to achieve its desired goal and ultimate success. While team members are fundamental for any organization, it is equally necessary that the company's vision is clear, and those on the team understand and see it. This is also known as the mission, the exact reason why the company exists. Having belief in the mission is also imperative for all team members, which would be the inner conviction to execute such abilities effectively and efficiently.

For the purpose for which we are called, each of us has a special anointing. We have a talent, an imparted gift which we use to perform and carry out God's purpose.

The body of Christ, which is a part of the kingdom of God, is comprised of members who have been gifted and anointed to carry out the great commission. Preceding his resurrection, Jesus told the disciples, *"All authority has been given to Me in heaven and on earth. Go therefore and make disciples of all the nations, baptizing them in the name of the Father and of the Son and of the Holy Spirit, teaching them to observe all things that I have commanded you; and lo, I am with you always, even to the end of the age. Amen."* (Matthew 28:18-20 NKJV).

Like an army, many of us are positioned and placed in areas to function according to our gift of ministry.

Within the church, there are those who are appointed as first apostles, second prophets, and thirdly teachers. Last but not least, are the works of miracles, the gifts of healing, the gift of help, and varieties of tongue. Gifts which are natural and spiritual, are both given by God. *A natural* gift is equivalent to an inherited talent, like singing, dancing, athleticism, or cooking. For *the spiritual gift*, when an individual is baptized (reborn) in Jesus, they receive it with the Holy Ghost.

On the day of Pentecost, Peter tells us what happens during the stages of rebirth. *"...let every one of you be baptized in the name of Jesus Christ for the remission of sins; and you shall receive the gift of the Holy Spirit."* (Acts 2:38b ᴺᴷᴶⱽ) The spiritual gift given is for equipping the saints, the work of ministry, and the edifying of the body. And as Jesus told the disciples to go ye out into the world, we have the gift, the talent, and the call of purpose to do so.

The gift of ministry no man can give
We are called the apostles for the Lord's word.

TODAY, YOU CAN SING THE LORD'S SONG "IN ONE ACCORD WE ARE STRONG
IN ONE MESSAGE WE SPEAK THE SAME"

Scripture Reference
♦ I Corinthians 12:28 ♦ Ephesians 4:11-12 ♦ Romans 12:5-8

I Want to Sing Your Song

Your Day's Reflection

_____

_____

_____

_____

_____

_____

_____

_____

_____

Part 3: The Chorus of Saints

Let the word of Christ dwell in you richly in all wisdom, teaching and admonishing one another in psalms and hymns and spiritual songs, singing with grace in your hearts to the Lord...
♦ **Colossians 3:12-16** NKJV

Brothers, if anyone is caught in any transgression, you who are spiritual should restore him in a spirit of gentleness. Keep watch on yourself, lest you too be tempted. Bear one another's burdens, and so fulfill the law of Christ.
♦ **Galatians 6:1-2** ESV

THE VERSE

For the grace of our Lord and Saviour Jesus Christ,
I kneel at this moment
and focus on that which is most pressing.
In the realms of intercession,
I sing for you, my brother.
I sing for you, my sister.

I sing to those whose wings have been clipped.
For you have soared high to toward the line with no limit.
You are not meant to be contained.
Or be chained against the ideals of the *what-ifs* and *hows*.

Your mission is

to esteem the message of glorious stars and light.

Shining ever so bright,
a city set on a high,
You are the salt of the earth to satisfy the flavour of God's Holy Shine.

By the grace of our Father's mercy,
and His unfailing love,
I sing the song of mended fences
to repair that which has been broken.
I know what it feels like to fall
and have no arms to lift you out.

I know what it feels like
to hug loneliness that refuses to let you go.

I know what it feels like
to weep the tears for the ones you love most.

In the name of Jesus Christ our Lord,
I sing to you, my brother.
I sing to you, my sister.
In the same fight,
our weapon is the force of love
that endures all things.

For the drummer, who lost their beat
because the devil has stolen your seat.
Never mind that which is past,
for great is the mercies of our Lord.
Unto everlasting, it is a balm upon the wounds burning with fire.
In the hoist of winds, the transformation begins.
He who makes all things new,
is right there in You.

Go forth, oh psalmist of praise.

Go forth, oh instruments of ten strings.

Win the good fight of faith.
for your smile, you shall reclaim.

To the scattered princes and princesses,
whose voices have shattered
from thrown stones of condemnations.

Be thou restored upon the pinnacle
for which Purpose has placed you.

The position is shaped for your stance
so, you can ride out storms
and sing the songs of heavens calls:
worthy for the cause.

To the Preacher man
whose heart has been attacked by perils of criticism.
There is now no condemnation to them in Christ,
so, arise from the dirt of pestilence and scorn.
He who started a good work in you,
shall complete it to the end.

To the grieved in spirit,
perplex by the seasons of unexplained deaths.
Cry on and shed your tears,
for God knows the root of all, you feel there.
He understands and will answer by and by.

For the grace of our Lord and Saviour Jesus Christ,
I kneel at this moment.
I am putting aside the strive.
I am putting aside the unforgiveness.
I focus on that which is most pressing and begin
to sing for you, my brother.

I Want to Sing Your Song

I sing for you, my sister.

My kindred of the Almighty Creator.
In the gathering, between our embrace,
is the bond of one body,
a chorus only we can sing.

YOUR SONG

For you my brother, For you my sister,
I sing the chorus
The chorus of love.

For you who is hurting
For you who is lost
I sing the chorus, of God's Grace.

For the Grace of Jesus Christ, the Lord.
I sing, sing to you.
I sing, I sing for you

For you my brother
For you my sister
I sing the Chorus
The chorus of love.

Reflection

Between friends, family, and our community and our world, one of the greatest gifts that anyone could ever receive is the embrace of compassion. With the act of love, and the hand of forgiveness, these are the elements that bridge and keep relationships together. The home, which is at the heart of society, is essential to how members are able to relate to one another. For everything we learn about who we are, stems from the members of our family who raise us. One of the founding principles that support people to stay strong together is believing in oneness. Like the human body, every member is intricately connected. For example, if you were to stub your toe accidentally, every fiber of your body – top to bottom- would feel it. Like compassion, and empathy, the body would feel the pain. Your hands would simultaneously reach down to hold your toe, as your eyes would weld up in tears, and your teeth would bite your lip. On the flip side, if you were to feel extremely happy, your lips would smile, and your eyes would sparkle with tremendous delight. Like the human body, in a collective sense, compassion is having the ability to feel other people's joy and pain.

With strive, it can often be the route for which division occurs in a relationship; nonetheless, it is the key for which people can understand the true meaning of forgiveness and unity.

From the fruit of the spirit to the gift of ministry, both ideals help guide and exhort the culture of oneness and unity. In 1 Corinthians 12, it details the diversities of spiritual gifts and how a human body might sound if there is division.

"If the foot should say, Because I am not a hand, I am not of the body, is it therefore not of the body? And if the ear should say, Because I am not an eye, I am not of the body, is it therefore not of the body? If the whole body were an eye, where would be the hearing? If the whole were hearing, where would be the smelling?" (I Corinthians 12:15-17 NKJV)

Singing, which is a significant ministry on its own, is significantly ingrained in how we express and relate to one another. In the genre of love songs, certain words are lyrically framed to say *"I love you"* and or *"forgive me."*

In the genre of gospel music, there are countless songs and hymns which address the internal and external conflicts of individuals and groups of people. Of the Christian culture, this type of singing is meant to teach and admonish people as they grow in Christ *"with grace"* in the "[heart] to the Lord."* (Colossians 3:12 NKJV).

The chorus of saints is symbolically to be the hand that reaches out to each other. Holding onto the faith it helps us to persevere in a world that is not our permanent home. With troubles at every hand and at any given moment, the word of God tells us that

"...if anyone is caught in any transgression, you who are spiritual should restore in a spirit of gentleness. Keep watch on yourself, lest you too be tempted. Bear one another's burdens, and so fulfill the law of Christ." (Galatians 6:1-2 ESV).

So, when we sing songs, it is not meant to cast judgement, or to make people feel ashamed. Nor is it to serve the purpose of throwing jabs of anger, but it is the melody of heaven transforming the hearts of men. The chorus that we sing is to create a bond within the body of Christ.

For the grace of our Lord and Saviour Jesus Christ... In the realms of intercession, I sing for you my brother. I sing for you my sister.... In the gathering. Between our embrace, is the bond of one body, a chorus only we can sing.

TODAY YOU CAN SING THE LORD'S SONG OF UNITY "FOR YOU MY BROTHER, FOR YOU MY SISTER, I SING THE CHORUS"

Scripture Reference
Colossians 3:12-16 ♦ Galatians 6:1-2 ♦ 1 Corinthians 12:15-17

Your Day's Reflection

_____

_____

_____

_____

_____

_____

_____

_____

_____

Jehovah Shalom, You
Are My Peace

Peace I leave with you, My peace I give to you; not as the world gives do I give to you. Let not your heart be troubled, neither let it be afraid.
♦ **John 14:27** NKJV
And the peace of God, which passeth all understanding, shall keep your hearts and minds through Christ Jesus ♦ **Philippians 4:7**

"How blessed are those who make peace! for they will be called sons of God.
♦ *Mattityahu (Mat) 5:9* CJB

THE VERSE

Jehovah Jireh (the Lord will Provide),
Jehovah Shamma (the Lord is here)
Jehovah Shalom, You are my peace.

Each time I step out the door, and come back,
I recognize that nothing guarantees of that which shall be.

To make it through one misery,
the peace for which I'd seek,
is not found in temporal substances,
but it is found in the essence of Your faithfulness.

In Your faithfulness,
there is a peace that no man can give.
It holds the heart to sustain the quality of strength.
For in the race toward the finish
it is needed to compel the mind to say,
"Yes, I can do it. Yes, I can make it."
In the embrace of a hug,
Peace is like the bliss never to end.

In house, on lands of wide expanse
happiness becomes the pace for which I can dance.
In the allure, I see no other truth
because there is no reason
to chase what is on the other side of the veiled allusion.

Everlasting father,
prince of peace,
coming to take the pain away.

There is a peace.
There is a wholesomeness.
There is a justice.
There is prosperity, contained in your hands.
It is the blessing which adds no sorrow.
It brings the definition of who we truly are in thee.

It is your reconciliation
given with the conviction to live.

Passing all understanding, it is the holding of hands
in the face of adversity and boundless storms.

It is the look of a father whose compassion gives support.

This peace that I pray for,
let it be in the container of my soul.

I Want to Sing Your Song

Let the peace overflow like oil in a glass
transparent with running over.

On the precipice of fragility,
may my mind settle on the horizon outlining the future.

Jehovah Jireh (the Lord will Provide),
Jehovah Shamma (the Lord is here)
Jehovah Shalom, You are my peace.

YOUR SONG

Jehovah shalom
you are my peace
Raging winds may blow
And wave arise

I'll stand still and know that you will fight for me.
I praise Jesus my prince of peace

Reflection

Like the taste of refreshing water, and like the warmth of sun-filled days, peace is that balm that washes over you, after long drawn out day. Within twenty-four hours, a lot can happen. From the moment you step out the door, there are little to big hurdles you have to jump over. Some of them are smooth sailing, while for others, you can barely make it. Through the traffic of people, cars, and the weather, there are varying situations that can bother you all at once. You have to wrestle with bills. You have to argue with your family members about this or that. You, yourself, have to grapple with your inner voice asking questions of, *how do I do this? How can I let this go? How can I move forward?* Louder and louder, your voice contemplates the issues from without and within. Not all of them are detrimental, but at times you do need a little peace to let you know that whatever is going on, you will be okay. And when peace comes, there is nothing that can make you feel more anchored and wholesome. It opens the way for there to be confidence. It creates an atmosphere for there to be understanding and reconciliation. It opens the door for new possibilities, and it does give you the strength to endure.

**There is a peace that passeth all understanding,
and the world cannot give it.**

When Jesus was about to leave the disciples, and the earth, He gave these words of comfort:

"Peace *I leave with you, My peace I give to you; not as the world gives do I give to you. Let not your heart be troubled, neither let it be afraid. You have heard Me say to you, 'I am going away and coming back to you.' If you loved Me, you would rejoice because I said, 'I am going to the Father,' for My Father is greater than I.*" (John 14:27-28 ^NKJV).

While Jesus would not physically be on the earth, he did give a glimmer of hope for when he would return. This peace He gave was a reassurance that while the disciples would have to abide in the earth until the "appointed time" they would have the strength, and grace given by God to make it through. The quality of such meant, they would gain the spiritual qualities and freedom to live. In the previous clause of John 14:27, Jesus had also said, he would send the "comforter" being the "Holy Ghost" which would teach and bring things to the disciple's remembrance (John 14:26).

Throughout the bible, peace is used to indicate a spirit of tranquility and freedom from...inward and outward disturbance [1]

In most cases, peace is the absence of conflict, and during the hard times, it becomes that embrace of grace to go through. It is the comfort to accept the changes as they come and accept what cannot be changed. Akin to *the quiet place*, it is the kind of calm that brings the silence after a long drawn out battle.

Oftentimes, peace can be hard to come by because between both sides of a fight, someone needs and wants to be right. But for the one who does seek for peace, they are the kind that *"shall be called the children of God"* (Matthew 5:6b).

While God is not opposed to going into battle, it is obvious from the beginning of time to present, He is the God who loves peace. Especially when it comes to his children.

With Jehovah Shalom, He gives you the confidence to persevere on your walk. He is the Prince of Peace, and the kind of peace he gives, no man can replicate or replace. Once you have His word to move on and go forth, you do not have to feel ashamed about what is behind.

Better things are ahead, and you have the priceless peace to lead you all the way.

Jehovah Jireh (the Lord will Provide),
Jehovah Shamma (the Lord is here)
Jehovah Shalom, You are my peace.

TODAY YOU CAN SING THE LORD'S SONG: "JEHOVAH
SHALOM, YOU ARE MY PEACE"

Scripture Reference
John 14:26-28 ♦ Philippians 4:7 ♦ Matthew 5:6,9

Your Day's Reflection

_____

_____

_____

_____

_____

_____

_____

_____

_____

Heaven Is Better Than This

*...And I saw a new heaven and a new earth: for the first heaven
and the first earth were passed away; and there was no more sea....
And God shall wipe away all tears from their eyes; and there shall
be no more death, neither sorrow, nor crying, neither shall there
be any more pain: for the former things are passed away.*
♦ **Revelation 21:1,4**

THE VERSE

If I showed you a better place,
And carried you there to receive you to Myself,
would you come?

Look around and see,
The wars
The rumours
The famine.
If I showed you a better place, would you come?

Now behold, set your sights toward the morning sky.
Set your affections on things above.
Visualize the possibility of a new birth.
be thee reminded of what this will all mean.

In your heart, the troubles arise, and they subside.

In your mind, the thoughts tumble about.
Which is why I the Lord warn in My Word, be
thou renewed. Be thou transformed
Behold, behold, I stand at your and knock.

Before you entered your mother's womb
I have always been fully aware of your struggles.
My thoughts toward you are never of evil.

I come, I come, knocking on your heart,
to shape it very well, in a new form.

Let it not be troubled.
Be not concerned.
I have come.
I have gone
to a place to prepare for you.

On paved roads made with gold.
in My House are the many places prepared for you.
It is not just words I say to entice,
or words I say to devoid you of your free will.
But it is to give you the blessed hope of my return.

I ask again,
if I showed you a better place,
And carried you there, receiving you as my own,
would you come?

Or is there something else.
Is this earth, what you treasure?
Is your hope set on earthen pleasures?

Hear the prophets, teachers and the Levites
Hear the words I bring to you
placed on tables in front of your enemy, the devil.

Alitta P.S Cadmus & Melissea M Walters

I have collected the broken pieces,
that were left to waste
for the elements of life to sweep it away.

Among the million,
the conclusion of the whole matter is quite simple.
In this New Jerusalem, My walls shall never break.
Built with precious stones,
it is the garnished foundation of eternity.

Your name written in the Lamb's book of life,
I will tabernacle with you forever.
Your tears shall be wiped,
and your sorrow will no longer abide.

The sickness of disease shall have no temerity.
The claws of death shall be cut off.
It shall never rule over you.

The sun and moon will have served their purpose
and My Glory is the Light.

If I tell you there is a place better than this,
and I will receive you as my own, will you come?

YOUR SONG

I want to go where the Angels sing
I want to go where my soul shall win
Eternal life
There's no more strife.
I want to go where my soul sits down
And all the pain is not around
I'am found
I'am sound

I want to go
where my Lord is king
And Jesus Christ is everything
He is the light
The Lamb, the light

Oh Heaven
The New Jerusalem
Is better than this,
Is Better than this

Oh Heaven
Oh Heaven
Is better than this
Is better than this
Oh Heaven
Oh Heaven
Better than this

Reflection

If someone were to tell you that *there is a better place than where you live,* would you want to stay or go? If someone were to say to you *this new place has streets like gold.* There are mansions for which you do not have to pay a mortgage, would you go? In this new place, your body is completely different, and there is absolutely no pain. You don't have to work. You don't have to worry about taxes. You don't have to worry about getting sick. If you could get to such a place, would you go? Or would you rather stay where things are "alright," and you do manage to get by. On top of that, there are breathtaking places that do make you feel divine and serene. If you had a choice, would you stay or go?

While this world is beautiful and has amazing undeniable qualities of the people and of nature, there is a place that is better than this.

Throughout history, time, and present-day teachings, there have been foretelling of a new heaven and a new earth. In song chorus and hymns, words like *"New Jerusalem"* and *"Promise Land"* hint of a new world that is vastly different from the one we live in now. Like an underground whisper, premonitions and warnings foretell how the world is going to change. Not just change, it will end.

Recorded in the book of Matthew, it is forewarned

"And you will hear of wars and rumors of wars... For nation will rise against nation, and kingdom against kingdom. And there will be famines, pestilences, and earthquakes in various places. All these are the beginning of sorrows" (Matthew 24: 6a,7-8).

Undoubtedly this raises a lot of fear, denial and unbelief because of how it will happen. For as the years come and go, and you abide until Jesus returns, you can't help but think about the things you want to accomplish. You think about those dreams you've had for a long time of living a fulfilled life. You even feel nostalgia about the good ole days when the world was a little better than it is *now*.

The signs which Jesus describes, pretty much spell disaster, and it can make anyone feel anxious. But in His conversation about His crucifixion, Jesus gave these words of comfort, *"Don't let yourselves be disturbed. Trust in God and trust in me. In my Father's house are many places to live. If there weren't, I would have told you, because I am going there to prepare a place for you... I will return to take you with me; so that where I am, you may be also..."* (Yochanan (John) 14:1-4 ᶜᴶᴮ).

John the apostle, known as the one whom Jesus loved (John 13:23) was given the profound revelation of things to come and a vision (preview if you will) about the new heaven:

"Then I saw a new heaven and a new earth, for the old heaven and the old earth had passed away, and the sea was no longer there. Also, I saw the holy city, New Yerushalayim, coming down out of heaven from God, prepared like a bride beautifully dressed for her husband" (Rev of Yeshua to Yochanan (Rev) 21:1-2 ᶜᴶᴮ).

Admittedly, the Lord has created everything beautiful in its time; however, it cannot be compared to what He has been preparing: Not only that: *"God shall wipe away all tears from [our] eyes; and there shall be no more death, neither sorrow, nor crying, neither shall there be any more pain: for the former things are passed away"* (Revelation 21:4). Satan and his kingdom will be vanquished, and the curse of death will forever be swallowed in victory. (Revelation 12:9). To get to the new heaven, the process begins with first believing in Jesus, and being reborn (through water baptism). When you are reborn, similar to your natural fathers last name, you have on the name of Jesus. Filled with the Holy Ghost, you are connected to God, and it becomes your (spiritual) passport to be raptured when Jesus returns to take you to be with him in eternity (forever). In this new place the cares of financial, health and other woes will be no more.

Occasionally when you look up and view the ambiance of the blue skies. Are you reminded of the new beginning that awaits you? If you could choose between the current life and the new, which one would you choose?

---

*If I were tell you there is a place better than this,
and I will receive you as my own, will you come?*

TODAY, YOU CAN SING THE LORD'S SONG: "OH
HEAVEN...THE NEW JERUSALEM..."

Scripture Reference
John 14: 1-3; 13:23 ♦ Revelation 1-3; 21:1-
2,4 ♦ 2 Peter 3:13 ♦ Matthew 24: 6-8

Your Day's Reflection

_____

_____

_____

_____

_____

_____

_____

_____

_____

In Your Song, Remember Me

Then beware, lest you forget the Lord who brought you out
of the land of Egypt, from the house of bondage.
♦ **Deuteronomy 6:12**

And He took bread, gave thanks and broke it, and gave it to them, saying,
"This is My body which is given for you; do this in remembrance of Me."
♦ **Luke 22:19**

THE VERSE

When you sing,
remember, I spoke the light.
Remember, I paved the way of existence,
established the earth and the entire universe.

I gave the land to man to till the ground,
and gave the woman a seed to be the body for the redeemed.
Out of bondage, were you delivered,
you once were enslaved
to build a city, not for me to dwell in.

In remembrance of Me,
take my body; break it,
and give thanks in your gatherings of unity.
Sing your song in the mornings and nights,

do it well, in the spirit of excellence.

Sing of my holiness
Sing of my righteousness
Sing of my leading
Sing of how I love thee
Show those not of this fold,
lost and burdened so.
Find them you must,
it is the greatest work you shall do.

When you are blessed by my hand,
while living in fields of flourishing promise lands,
until I come,
feed my sheep.
Love them as you love Me.

Do not let it be a doctrine for mankind to think,
I am a man that tells lies.
Let them know I am the Lamb
slain from the foundations of the earth.

Keeping my promise of the victory given to conquerors.
I am the true vine, and ye are the branches.

Arise from the slumbers of your sleep.
Stand in the center of prosperity.
Dress in the clothes washed for your soul.
Where it well sparklingly in white.

In your songs of timbrel and dance.
In your song of hallelujahs and praise
Beat the drums of joy, happiness and gladness.
The fullness of joy is found in my presence,
and at my right hand, there are pleasures forevermore.

In the devotions of your prayers,
In your deliverance; even in your pain,
In all, you say and do.
When you cross over this Jordan,
in your song, remember me.

YOUR SONG

I will sing to remember you.
I will sing your song
I will sing to remember the days,
of how you saved me by your grace

I will sing
I will sing
I will sing to remember you. (Sing to remember you)
I will sing your song

Sing the Song of Remembrance

What has the Lord done for you yesterday.
What shall He do for you tomorrow?
For the blessing.
For the healing.
For the deliverance.
For redemption of sin remember Him in your song.

"…Remember this day in which you came out from Egypt, out of the house
of slavery, for by a strong hand the Lord brought you out from this place…
(Exodus 13:3a-b ᴱˢⱽ)

TODAY YOU CAN SING YOUR SONG OF REMEMBRANCE TO THE LORD.

Scripture Reference
Deuteronomy 6:12 ♦ Luke 22:19

Your Day's Reflection

_____

_____

_____

_____

_____

_____

_____

_____

_____

The Song of Gratitude

Speaking to yourselves in psalms and hymns and spiritual songs, singing and making melody in your heart to the Lord; Giving thanks always for all things unto God and the Father in the name of our Lord Jesus Christ.
♦ **Ephesians 5:19-20**

THE VERSE

My song of gratitude is the gold diamond,
I wish to display in my heart.
With the harmony align right,
it is me, Oh Lord,
Your worshipper giving back to you.

The days have come and finished their course.
Along the way, I slipped and cracked.
Picking me up, you kept my dignity intact
so that I could lift my head and stand.

With a heart of gratitude,
I acknowledge the grace you have given
for my soul to cross the marathons' distance.

Forming prostrate of humility,
I close my eyes and recognize the face of the light.

These many things, I think.
These many things, I say.
These many things, I do.
Out of them all, I must remember to say thank you.

Thank you, Jesus, for the peace to stand in storms.
Thank you, Jesus, for the power of your blood.
Thank you, Jesus, for the breaking of bread.
Thank you for another chance.

When I should be left alone
to face my orchestrated calamity,
You have set my foot on the right path.
Turning it around for my good, I can live again.

These things, I say, and do,
for the precious name of Jesus,
this is my song of Gratitude.

YOUR SONG

These things I say and do, Is all because of you
These things many things I think,
Out of them I must remember.
For your love you give to me, I can sing my liberty

I will sing
I will sing
Oh Lord, your song, my gratitude
I will sing
I will sing
Your song, my gratitude

Sing the Song of Gratitude

One of the lepers return to say thank you, and he received his healing. *Have you returned to say thank you?* For this brand-new morning of second chances, have you told Him *how much you appreciate Him?* For the roof over your head. For watching while you sleep. For not forgetting about you when all others have walked away, *have you turn back to say thank you?*

"…Speaking to yourselves in psalms and hymns and spiritual songs, singing and making melody in your heart to the Lord; Giving thanks always for all things unto God and the Father in the name of our Lord Jesus Christ; (Ephesians 5:19-20)

TODAY YOU CAN SING YOUR HEART'S SONG OF GRATITUDE TO THE LORD

Scripture Reference
♦ **Ephesians 5:19-20**

_____

_____

_____

_____

_____

_____

_____

_____

_____

The Song of Repentance

If My people who are called by My name will humble themselves, and pray and seek My face, and turn from their wicked ways, then I will hear from heaven, and will forgive their sin and heal their land.
♦ **2 Chronicles 7:14**

THE VERSE

I have walked in the wrong way.
I have sin in your sight.
I thought I could hide,
and still, be found worthy in your courts.

For the times I have taken your mercy for granted.
Mocking your grace and having no heart of conviction.
On my knees, I come, with the humbleness required.

Words from the mouth are not enough.
Saying *"I'm sorry"*, does not equate to the turning of the soul.
It is the complete turning around and leaving that which is behind.
Lying flat on my face, I seek for forgiveness.

Choosing you this day,
with my body being your temple,

wash me from without and within.
Create in me a clean heart, for thou desirest truth.
Thou desirest true worship.

Praying in my song.
Called by Your name Jesus.
Lord of true holiness.

I turn, I turn from my wicked ways.
I turn and understand that true repentance
is what you desire, in the songs we lay on your altars.

Division must not be found amongst your children.
Upon the seat of grace, we must leave our gifts and make it right.
For you cannot bear when there is strife.
It is a choice on both hands.

I pray,
I pray,
beseeching for the strength to win the fight.
Praying in my song
Called by Your name
Lord of true holiness, I turn from my wicked ways.

YOUR SONG

Praying in my song, all the day long.
Seeking your face in the quiet place,
Lord Holy and true, I bow down in reverence.
I bow down in repentance.
With the chasten heart I turn from my ways
And point my feet to walk in the narrow way.

More than an apology
Clean my heart Oh Lord

So that I can walk whole
Holy you are
Let not my sins keep us far apart.

I will sing
I will sing
The song of true repentance.

Sing the Song of Repentance

David was a man after God's own heart because when he was wrong, he repented from his ways with conviction. When you have fallen. When you have made your mistakes. The guilt may weigh you down, but it is the "*broken spirit*" and "*contrite heart*" He will not turn away (Psalm 51:17). True repentance is the turning of the heart unto righteousness.

If My people who are called by My name will humble themselves, and pray and seek My face, and turn from their wicked ways, then I will hear from heaven, and will forgive their sin and heal their land.
(2 Chronicles 7:14 NKJV)

TODAY YOU CAN SING YOUR HEART'S SONG OF REPENTANCE TO THE LORD

Scripture Reference
2 Chronicles 7:14 ♦ Psalm 51:17

Your Day's Reflection

Your Song of Melody

*All the earth bows down to you, sings praises to
you, sings praises to your name.*" (Selah)
♦ **Tehillim (Psa) 66:4** CJB

*O sing unto the Lord a new song: sing unto the Lord, all the earth. Sing
unto the Lord, bless his name; shew forth his salvation from day to day.
Declare his glory among the heathen, his wonders among all people.*
♦ **Psalms 96:1-3**

THE VERSE

To the God of heavenly truth:
Let this voice sing Your melody right.
Let it be whole.
Let it be the harmony, blended as one in praise and glory.
Let it be on one accord with the expression of worship.

Spirit of inspiration,
Liberator of the suppressed, and distressed,
You have placed the power on my tongue
to release the sweetest sounds for the valley of dry bones.

In graves for those who sleep,
You give the song of rest,
for they shall awake in Christ arising to meet you in the air.

I Want to Sing Your Song

I sing for that day.

I sing for the rock upon which I can stand.

I want to sing your song
I want to sing your melody
I want to sing about your love
I want to sing of your holiness.

Not of stubborn cultures.
Not of strange fires
Not of self-glory.

Let it be whole.
Let it be right.

Textured by the bellow of the anointing,
Leaving that which is behind,
I sing the new song, the anthem for saints.
I sing the new chorus, for children of generations to come.
I sing, I sing, the song of God's love.

I sing the song of visions
I sing your song of prophecies
I sing your song of release.
I sing you are God, Jesus Christ, the Lord.
My song of eternal glory
I sing your song, the authentic culture of heaven.

YOUR SONG

I want to sing your song
I want to sing your melody
I want to sing about your love
I want to sing of your righteousness

I want to sing your holy
I want to sing faithful
I want to sing your song

I want to sing your merciful
I want to sing your wonderful

I want to sing your song
I wanna (x2)
I want to sing your song

Sing the Song of Melody

The anthem of Heaven is to sing about God's Love. The anthem of Heaven is to sing about God's truth. The anthem of Heaven is to sing of His Holiness. The Anthem of Heaven is to sing about the oneness in Christ. The anthem of Heaven is to sing the new song a melody done right.

Sing unto him, sing psalms unto him: talk ye of all his wondrous works.
(Psalms 105:2)

TODAY YOU CAN SING YOUR NEW **SONG OF** MELODY UNTO THE LORD

Scripture Reference
Psalm 66:4 ♦ Psalms 96:1-3 ♦ Psalm 105:2 ♦

Your Day's Reflection

_____

_____

_____

_____

_____

_____

_____

_____

_____

You Are My Great Change

*He put a new song in my mouth, a song of praise to our God. Many will look
on in awe and put their trust in Adonai.* ♦ **Psalms (Tehillim) 40:4** ^{CJB}

THE VERSE

Because of you, I understand The intimacy of praise and worship.
Because of you, I can sing the song of Joy for every season.
Because of you, I Sing in my quiet Place.
With your Holy Spirit raining down on me,
I can abide, and "just" be in your presence.

Because of you, I can call your name Jesus.
For the days when I look to find thee,
I am careful to know who you are to me.
It is a conviction to understand and believe when you speak.
*Oh Lord, let your word abide in me, so that I
may sing Your songs of sweet melody*

Possessed in your reverence, I 'am here without apology.
Designed with the structure to be, my body is Your Temple.
Renewed in the spirit of my mind,
I can walk in the spirit, bearing good fruit.

Troubles and cares have come.
In the loneliness, you remind me that you are always there.

At your feet, I can lay my burdens down.
With my faith, I can make it all the way.
Trusting you, I know you'll keep me up with your unfailing grace.

In these prayers, I tell the truth.
Giving my supplications, I hope for what you will do.
Becoming the new creature, I will not look back.
For it is your Perfect Love that keeps me pressing on.
Drinking from your fountain, I will never thirst.
And when I fall and rise, I can smile again.

Pursuing that which has been stolen,
I put on the whole armour of God,
for You have not given me the spirit of fear.

Because you are our strength,
we have the power, we have the victory.

Called to the purpose,
with the gift of ministry,
in the saints' army,
I can sing the Holy chorus.
We are one body

With the peace you give, which no man can take away.
I know one day; I'll dwell in Heaven that is better than this.

In my songs, I remember you.
Never forgetting to be grateful for all you do
Repenting of sins and transgression.
With a clean heart, I can sing your song.

For you are my great change

YOUR SONG

You my great change,
Your great change
Whatever you want me to do
Lord I will live for you
Storm clouds may rise
But in your Word, I 'll hide
I will worship at your feet
You are my
You are my great change.

Sing the Song of a Great Change

Praise the Lord Jesus for what He has done. He is my God. He is my King. I will forever dwell in God's presence and find the fullness of joy and pleasures forevermore. He is the reason why I can sing His Song. He has given the rhythm of heaven. Sitting at the well, He waited for me, and now I can tell the people of how He transformed me. He is my great change.

He put a new song in my mouth; a song of praise to our God. Many will look on in awe and put their trust in Adonai. (Psalms (Tehillim) 40:4 ᶜᴶᴮ)

TODAY YOU CAN SING YOUR SONG OF A GREAT CHANGE UNTO THE LORD

Scripture Reference
♦ **Psalm 40:4**

Your Day's Reflection

_____

_____

_____

_____

_____

_____

_____

_____

_____

The Cross Over

It is time to walk out the door and cross over.
This is your moment of verse and song.
It's time to step into the glass shoes of transparency
and shine on the path written for humanity.

It is not to boast
or to wear the mask of pride and arrogance.
But it is to imprint the vision on the minds of those
still sitting in the seat of hallow places.
They are still sitting in the seat of the yearning for something different.
They are still sitting in the seat of broken chairs.

It's time to cross over and finish the *verse and song*
God has given from days past and gone.

He has given you the valley
He has given you the mountain
He has given you the pain
He has given you the tears
He has given you the balm

The frame is set for your portrait
And the deconstruction of your image has been made a new
This is your verse and song
Go
Go
Go and
Finish it.

About The Authors

A poet, song, and fictional writer, ALITTA P.S CADMUS, has written and performed several poems that speak to the heart, mind, and soul. Her first performance, "What can I name this" in 2008, received resounding reviews, which later launched her to write several more poems. 2018 she was a featured performer at Talks with Sosa in support of the communal discussion about addiction and mental awareness. Her two written pieces (Escaping the Unwanted; Accepting the Wanted & Her Story: My life) received astounding reviews and appreciation for its social context and relatability.

Dedicated to the cause of spiritual, emotional, and mental health, most of Alitta works identify and underline the issues that she has personally experienced. An advocate for the arts, she employs the use of creative license to minister God's word in a relatable way. Through her own company (Capsonart), she has co-authored I Want to Sing Your Song (Daily Devotional) with her sister Melissea M. Walters. Currently, Alitta resides in British Columbia Canada with her family and is involved in the evangelical ministry at her local church Bethel United. A recent graduate from Kwantlen Polytechnic University, Alitta is focused on her next fictional project while campaigning and building mental awareness through the ministry of creative arts.

MELISSEA M WALTERS is a woman of God who aspires to serve in the Kingdom of God. Dedicated to the ministry, born in Canada and raised in the church, she has grown into a song lyricist with the anointed ability to blend voices in harmony. Appointed by God, she wrote and performed her first song "Nobody but Jesus" during a Christmas concert at her local church in Toronto. Married to the love of her life, Minister Joshua Walters, they both have the gift to sing for God while expounding on the gospel of healing and restoration. Through community outreach, Melissea and her husband currently work together in ministry writing devotionals, teaching and serving in Edmonton and the surrounding metropolitan area. Alumni of George Brown College and Kwantlen Polytechnic University, her field of work focuses on social support within her local community. Partnered with her sister, Melissea continues her work in the ministry of reconciliation.

To learn more about Alitta P.S Cadmus and Melissa M Walters visit www.alittacad.wixsite.com/capsonart

Notes

You Give Me Joy

1. Vaughan, Cadmus, R, Marie. *Roses Among Thorns: Flourishing in the Midst of Adversity.* 1 ed. Surrey, BC: Capsonart. 2020. https://read.amazon.ca/kp/embed?asin=B082ZDW4LC&preview=newtab&linkCode=kpe&ref_=cm_sw_r_kb_dp_KufoFbW33DPR1

The Quiet Place

1. Strong, J. The New Strong's Concordance: Exhaustive Concordance of the Bible (Nashville, Tennessee: Thomas Nelson Publishers, 1990), 116
2. Ibid, 120
3. Ibid, 117

Renewed in the Spirit of My Mind

1. Mars, Michelle and Oliver Meegan. "Mindfulness is more than a buzz word: Towards a sustainable model of health care." *Journal of the Australian Traditional-Medicine Society* 22, no. 1 (2016): 7–10 https://ezproxy.kpu.ca:2443/login?url=https://search.ebscohost.com/login.aspx?direct=true&db=ccm&AN=114257336&login.asp&site=ehost-live&scope=site
2. Ibid, 8

The Walk of Thy Statues

1. Cadmus, Vaughan R Marie. "Walking in the New Life" *Bethlehem United Churches in Canada* National Rationale 2017 1-3

Bear Good Fruit
1. Deanna Conners, "Why trees shed their leaves," EarthSky (blog), Nov 8, 2017, https://earthsky.org/earth/why-do-trees-shed-their-leaves

By Prayer and Supplication
1. *Holman Study Bible.* King James Version. (Holman Bible Publishers) 2012. 1991-1992

Part 1: I'am Walking in a Brand-New Life
1. Websters English Dictionary: Concise Edition. For school, home, and office. (1999). Geddes & Grosset. David Dale House, Landmark Scotkand. 206
2. Deanna Conners, "Why trees shed their leaves," EarthSky (blog), Nov 8, 2017, https://earthsky.org/earth/why-do-trees-shed-their-leaves

I Can Smile Again, for I 'am Blessed
1. Sarah Stevenson, "There's Magic in Your Smile: How smiling affects your brain." *Psychology Today* (blog) June 25, 2012. https://www.psychologytoday.com/ca/blog/cutting-edge-leadership/201206/there-s-magic-in-your-smile

The Whole Armour of God
1. "Rules of Engagement" Encylopedia Briticanna Revised by Melissa Petruzzello, 2016. https://www.britannica.com/topic/rules-of-engagement-military-directives
2. Stevenson, "There's Magic in Your Smile: How smiling affects your brain"

You Are My Strength
1. Websters English Dictionary: Concise Edition. For school, home, and office. (1999). Geddes & Grosset. David Dale House, Landmark Scotkand. 326
2. Deborah Schoeberlein David "A Thin Line Between Love and Hate" *HuffPost* (blog) December 9, 2016 https://www.huffpost.com/entry/a-thin-line-between-love_b_8758034

Jehovah Shalom, You Are my Peace
1. *The Compact Bible Dictionary.* (1967) edited by T. Alton Bryant. Zondervan Publishing House. 443